STABLE OF HORSES

PICTURE BOOK

VOL. 3

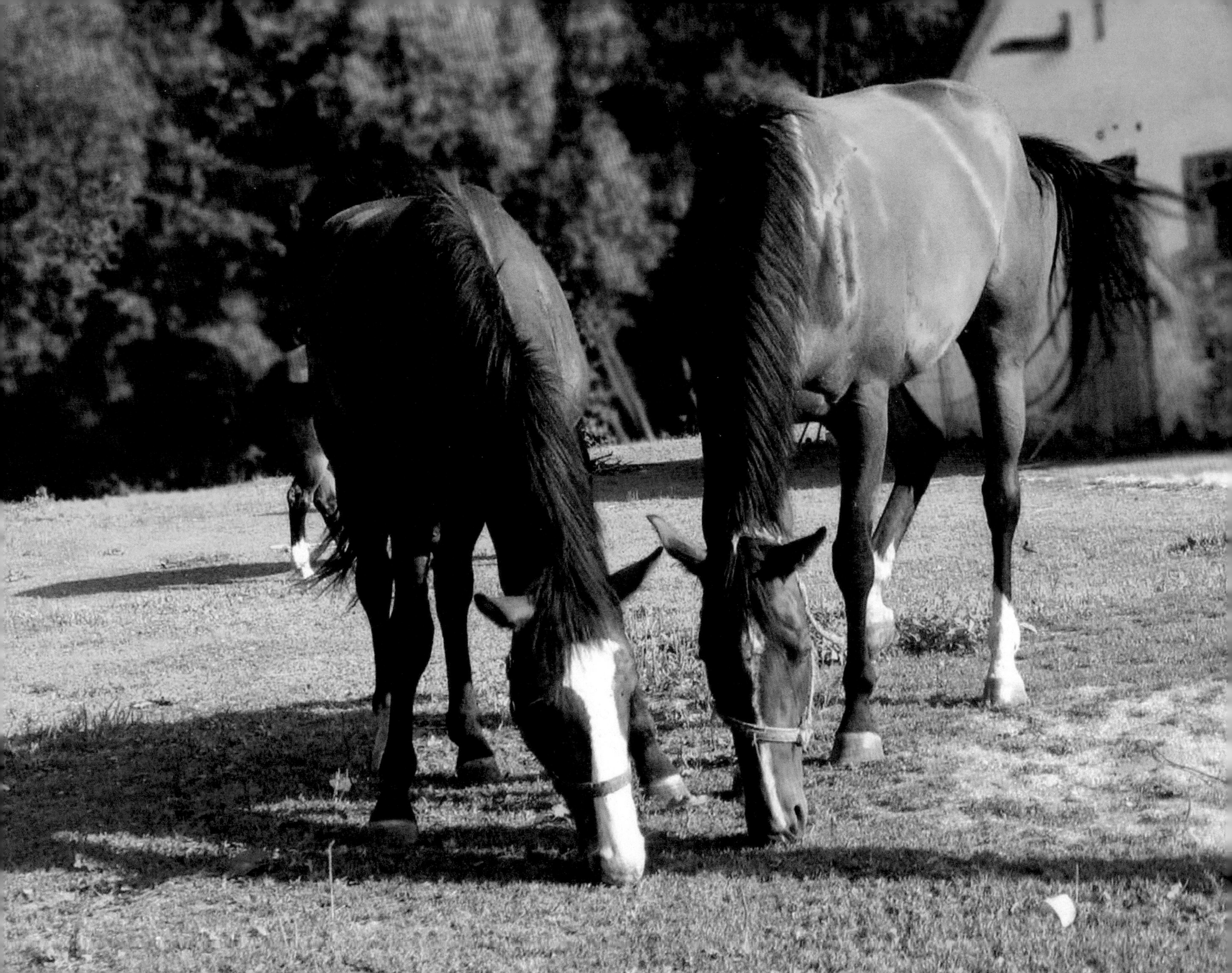

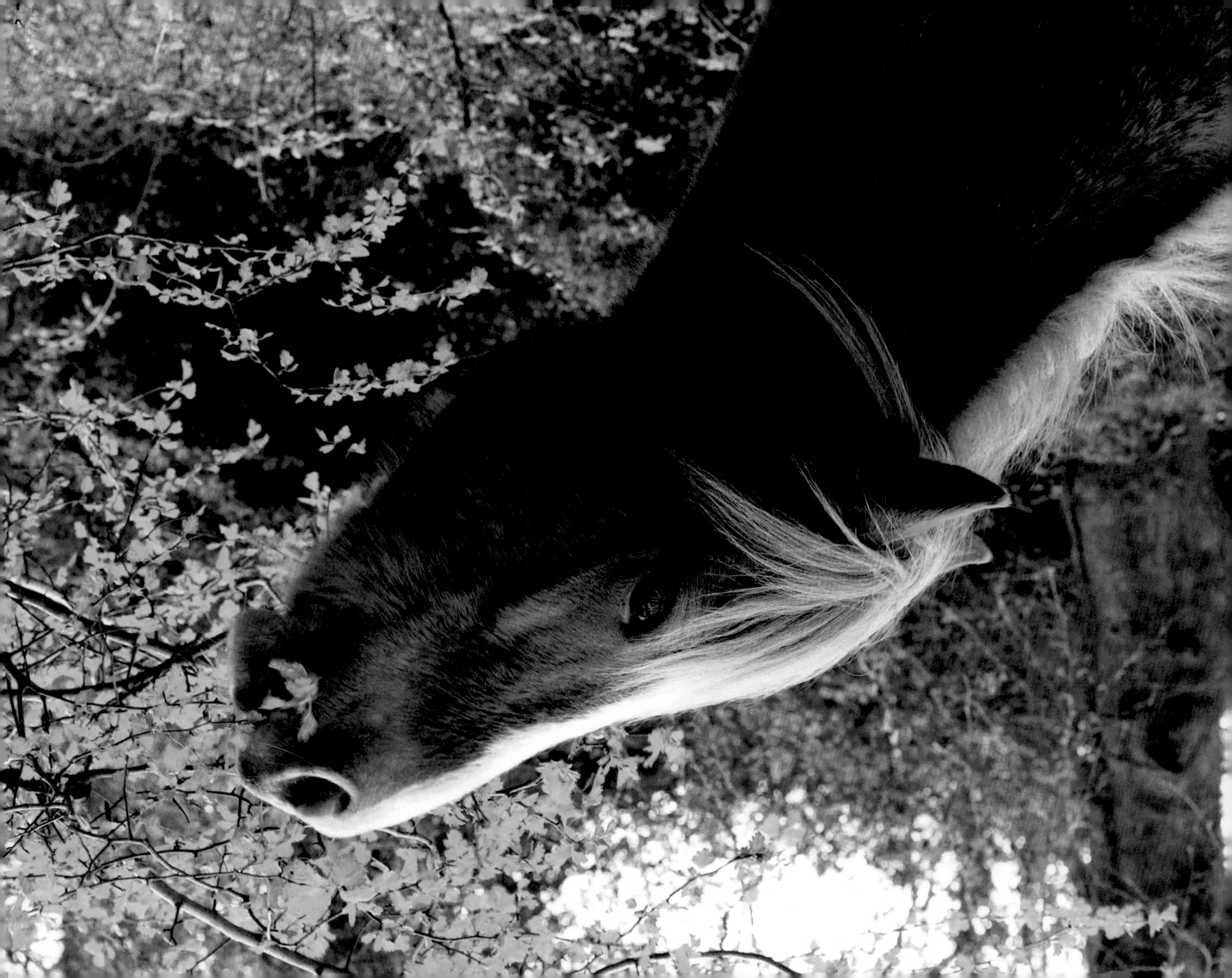

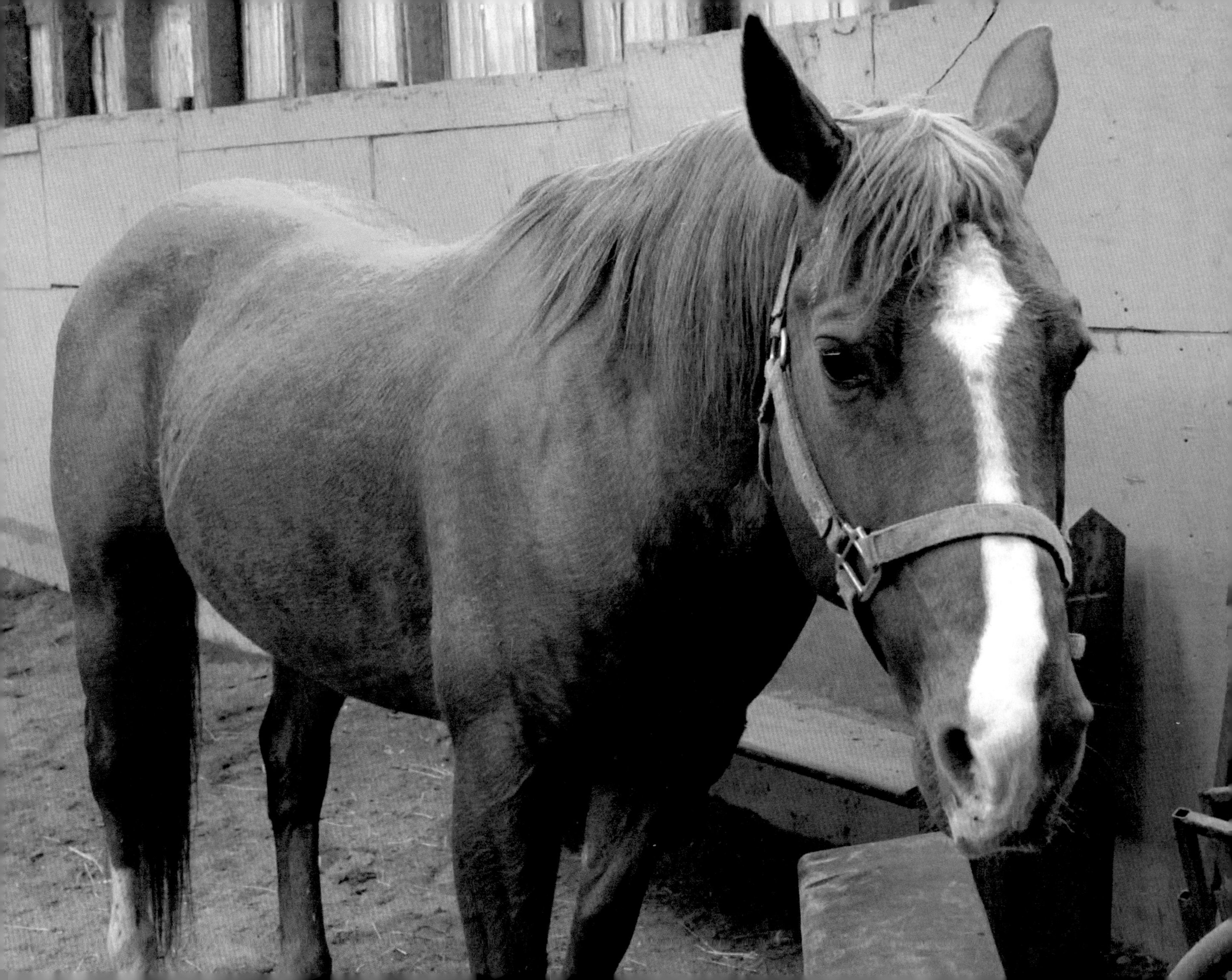

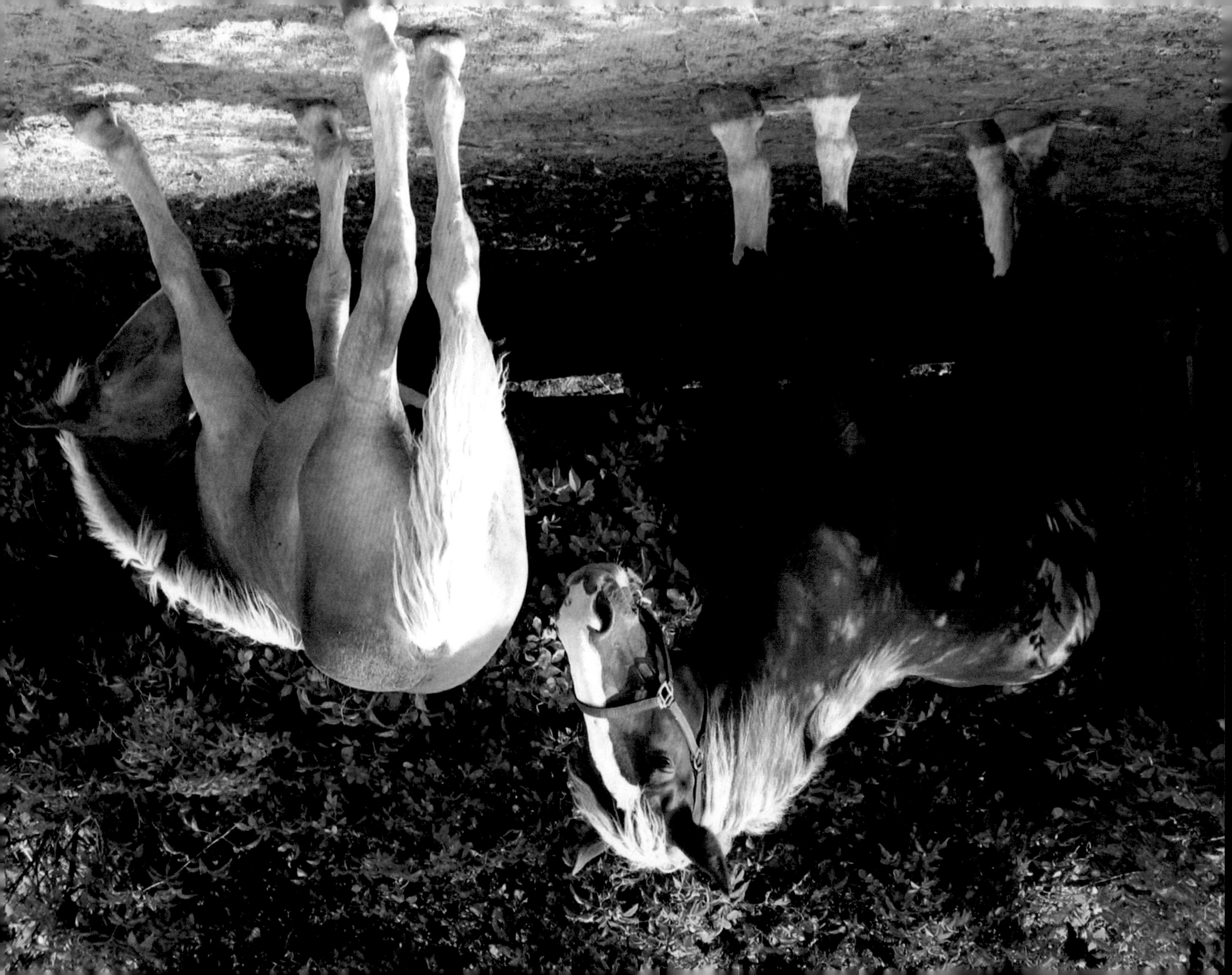

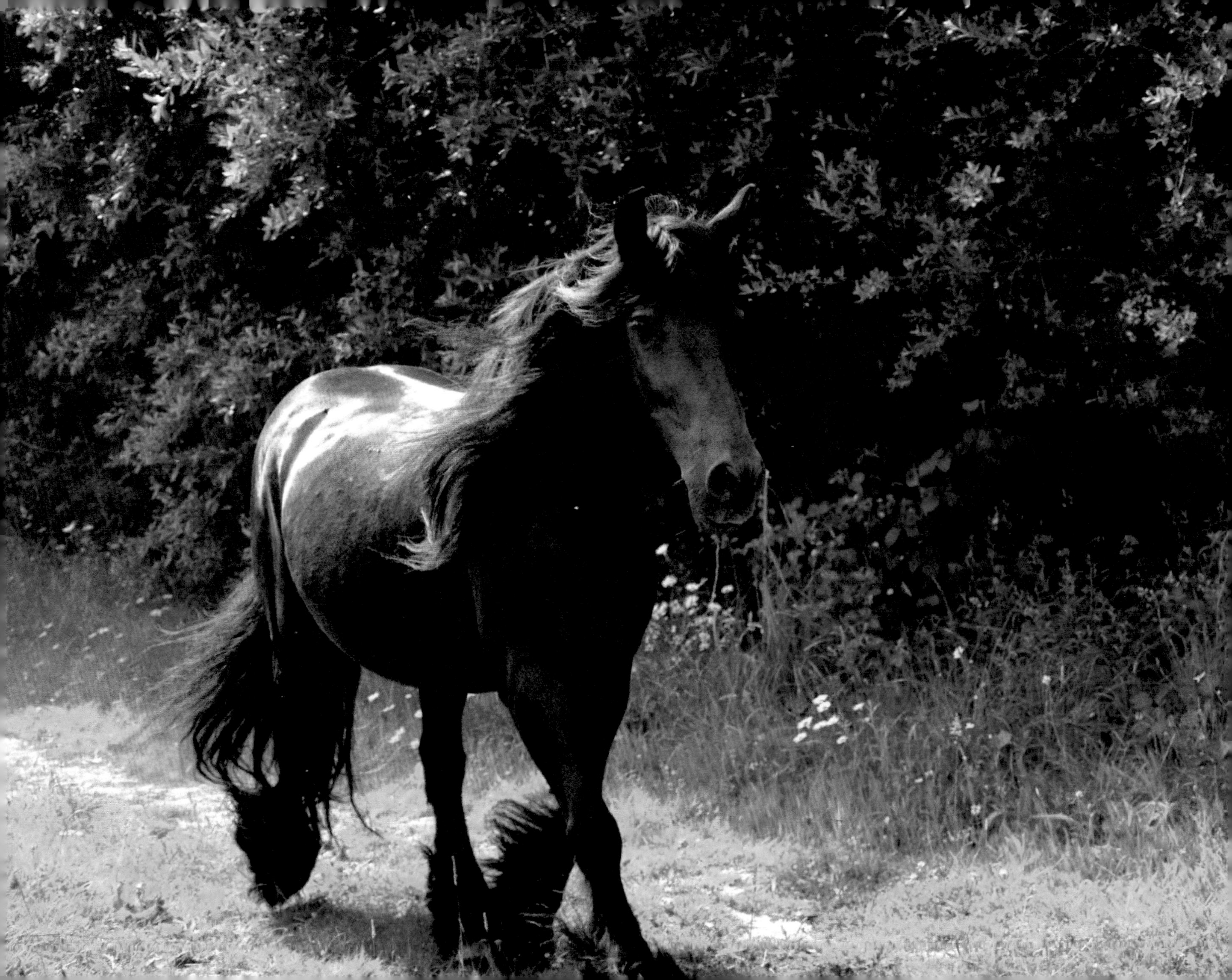

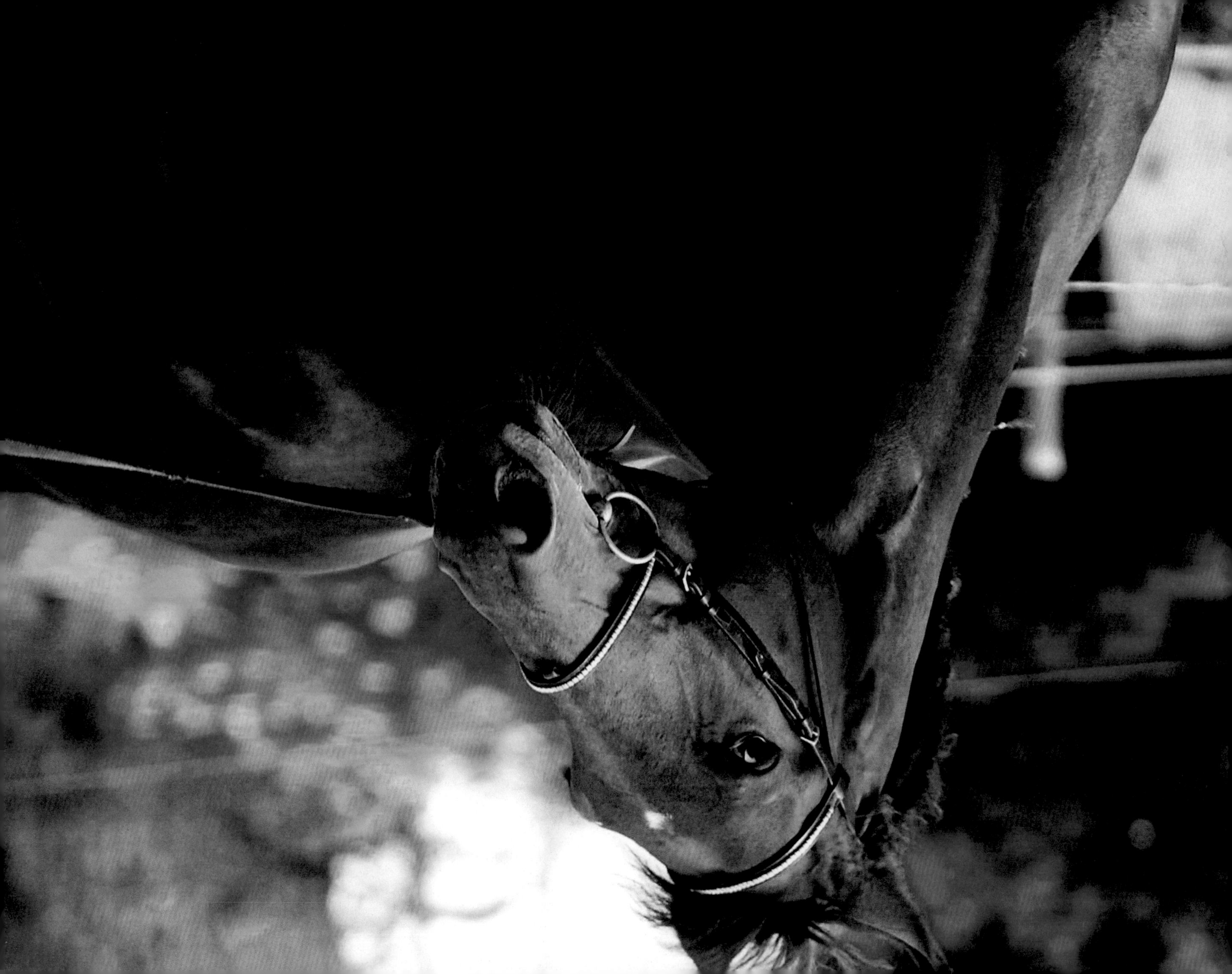

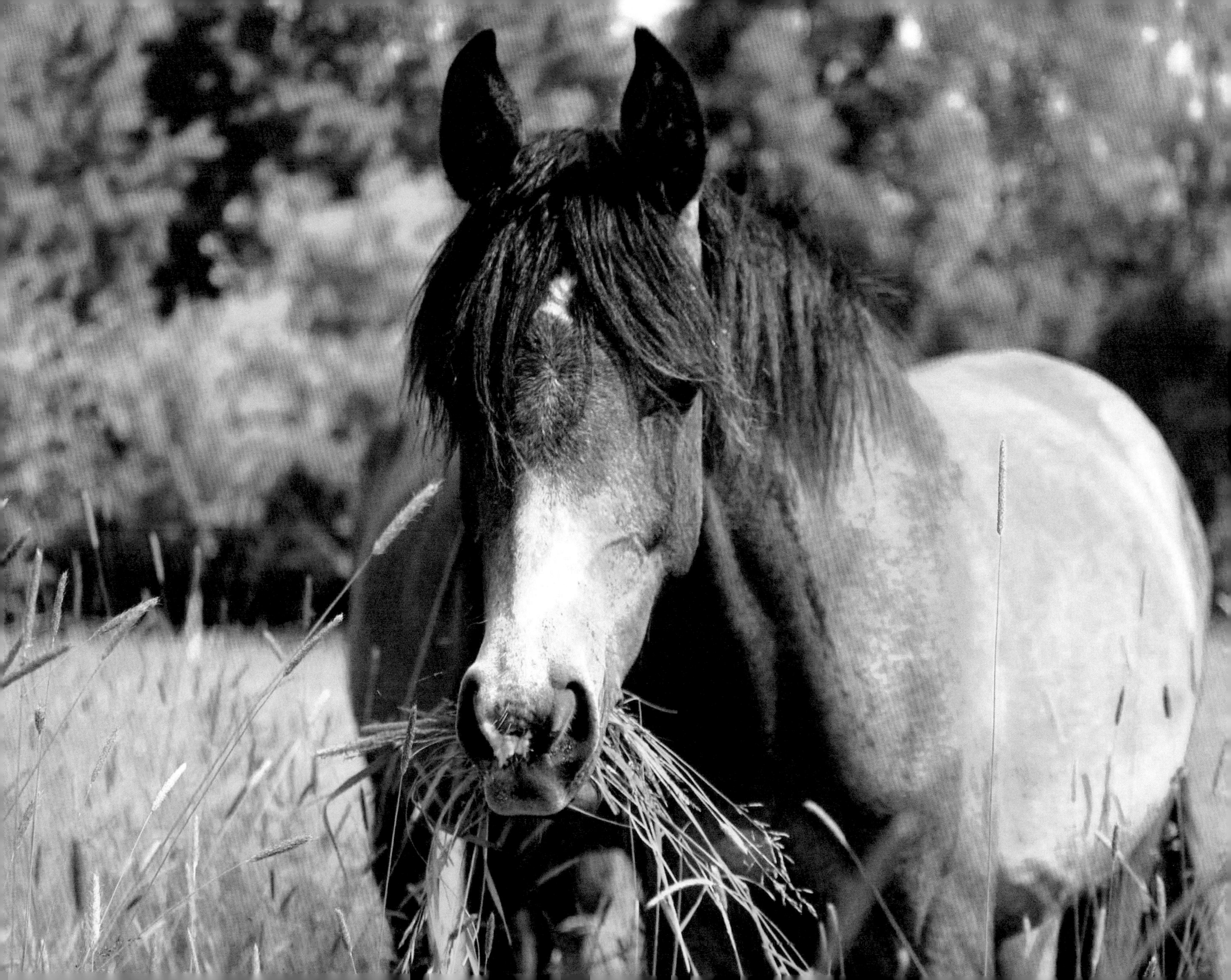

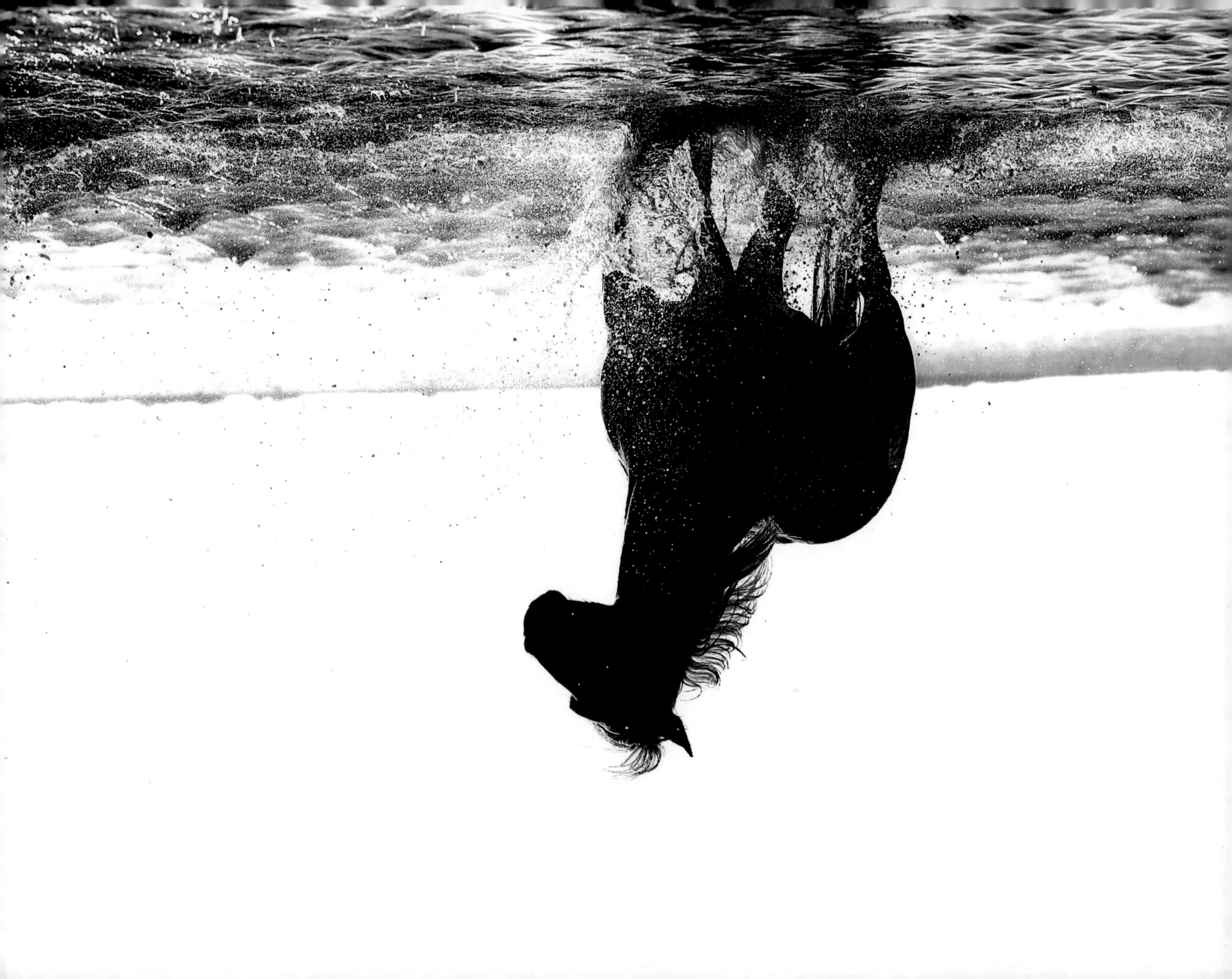

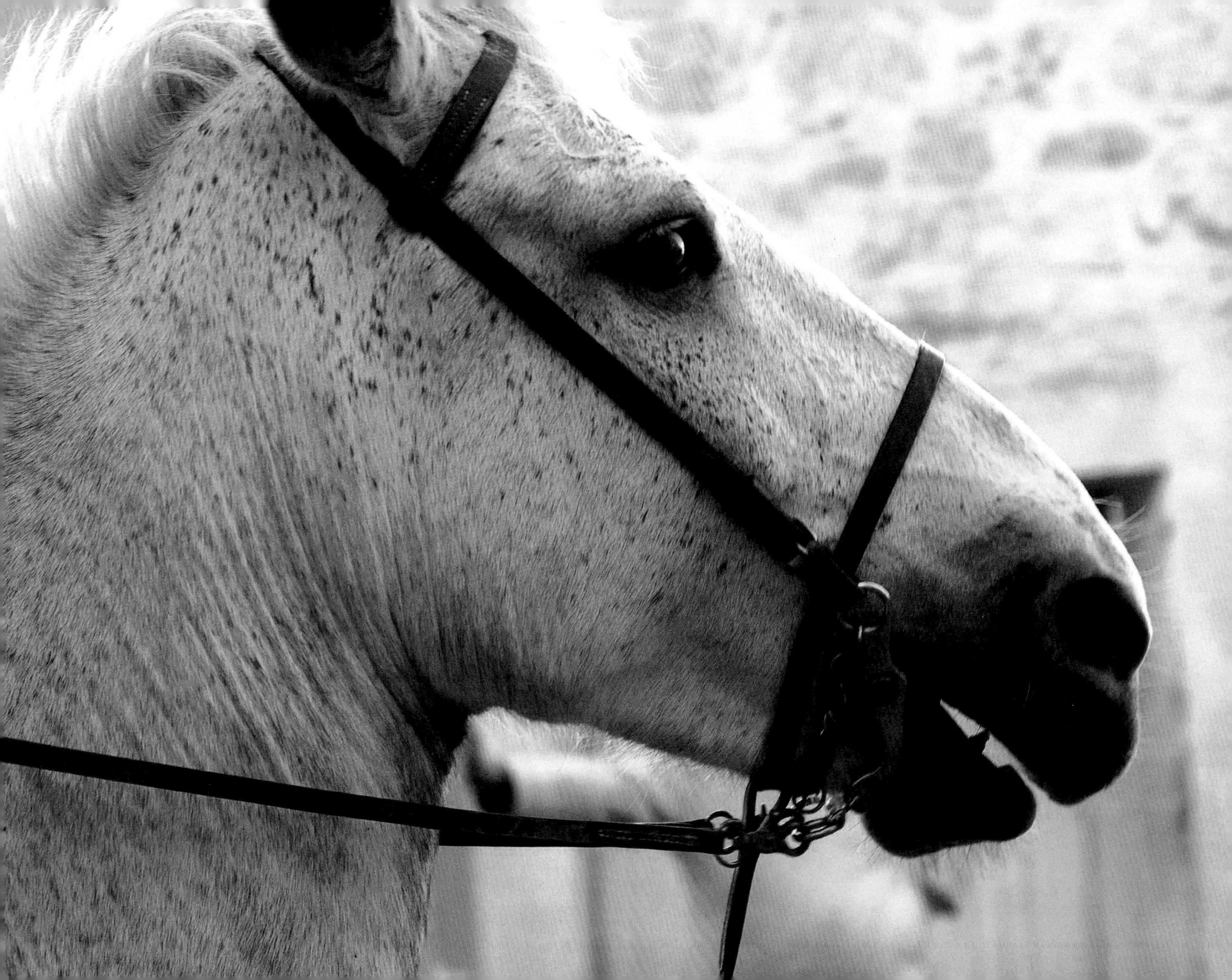

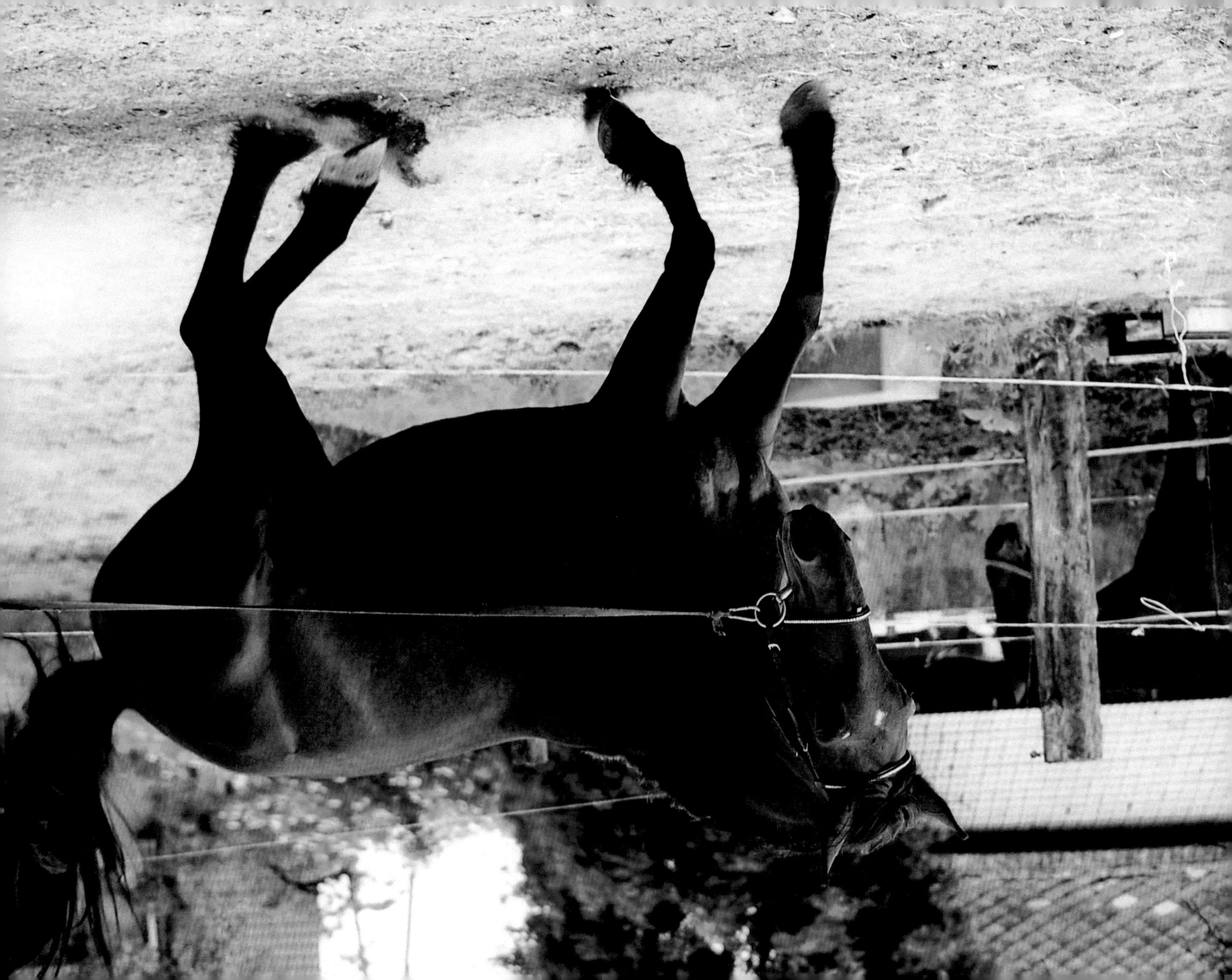

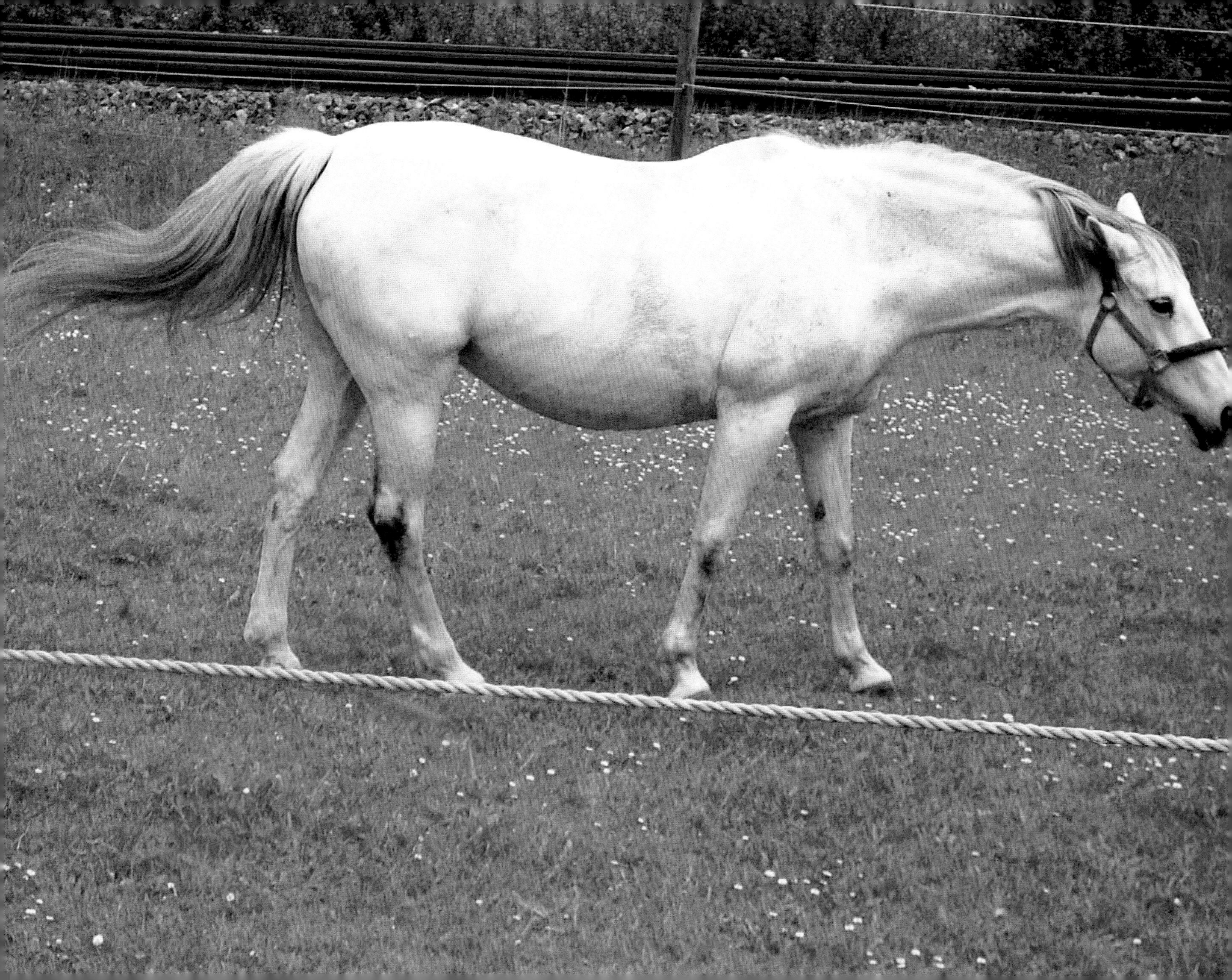

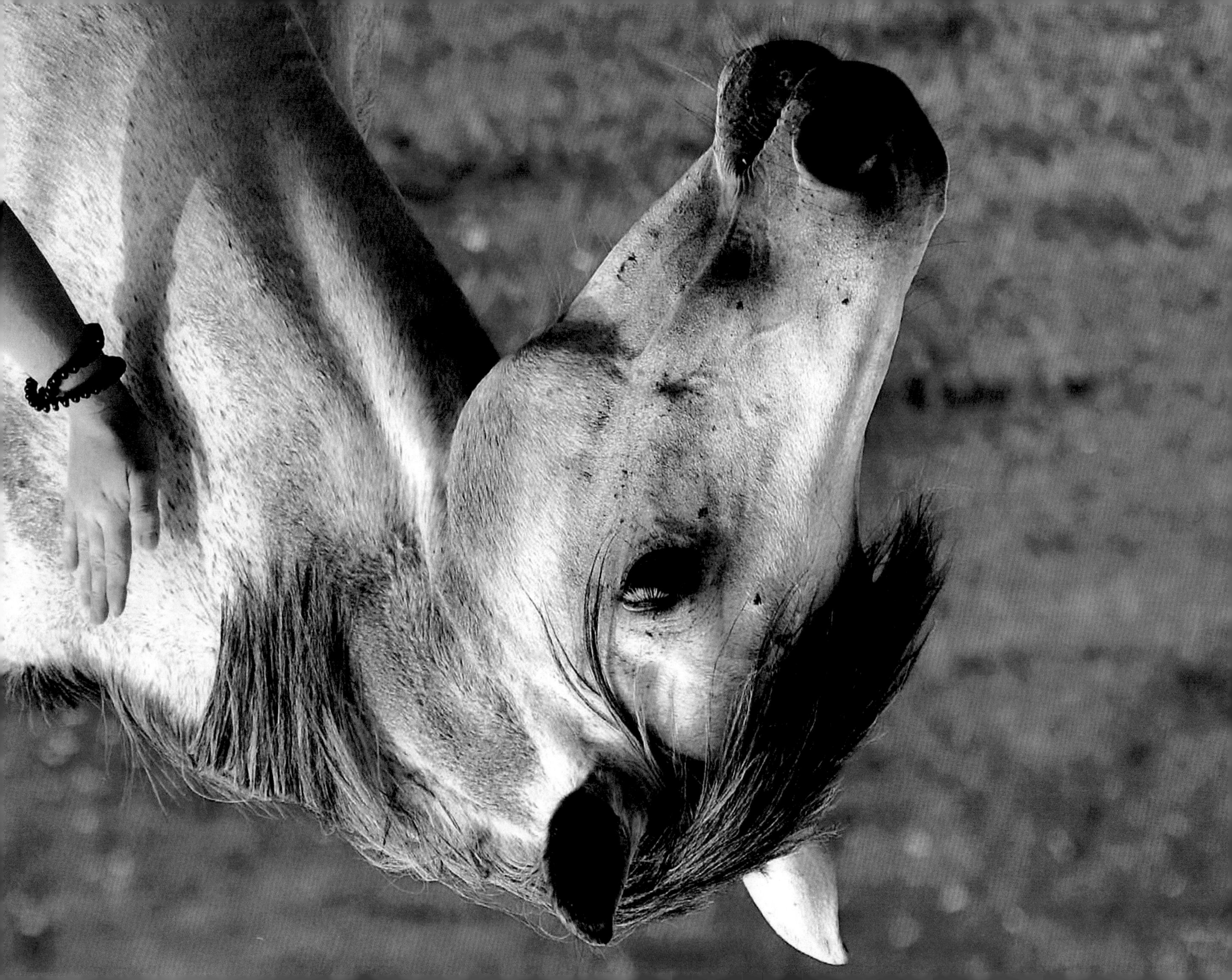

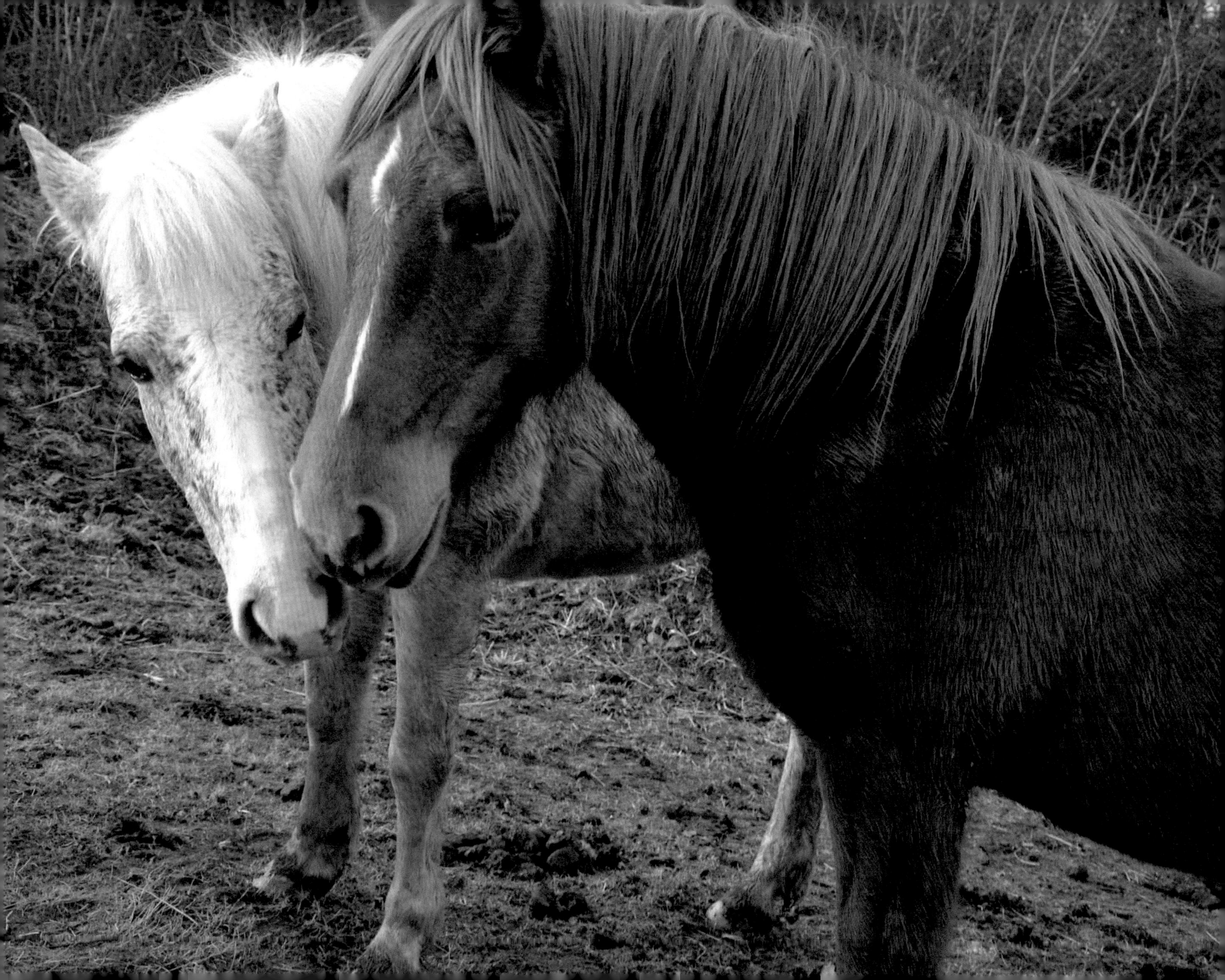

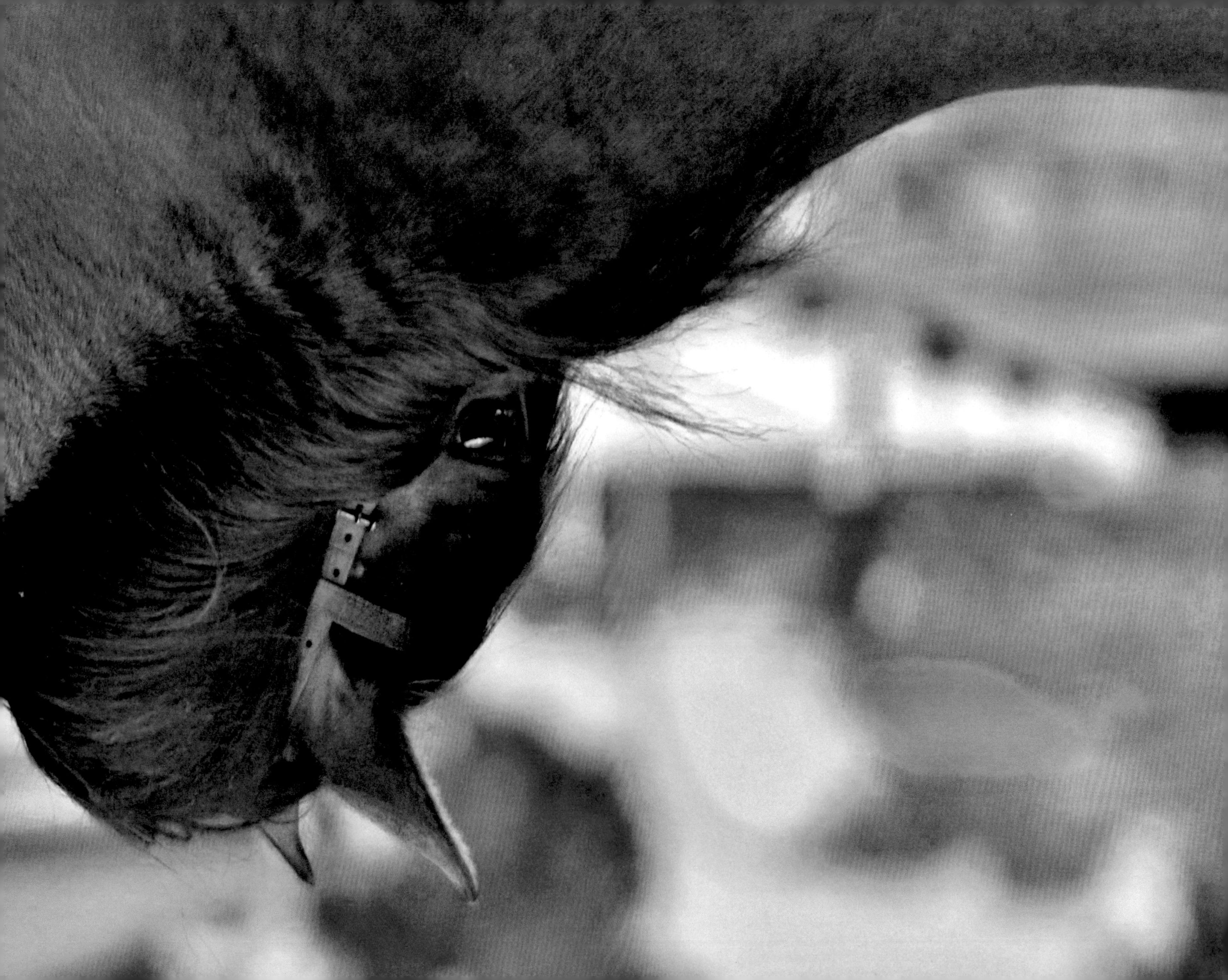

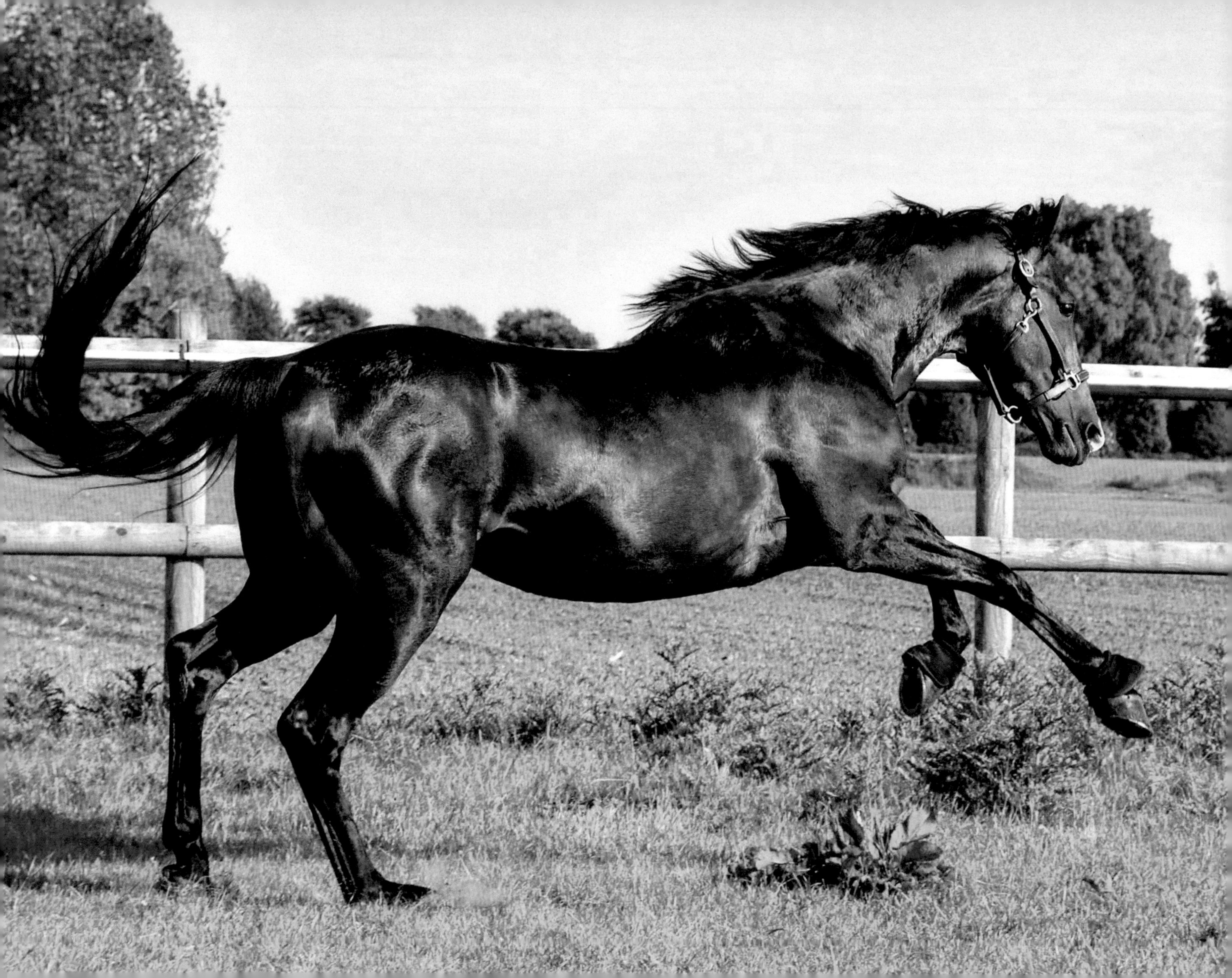

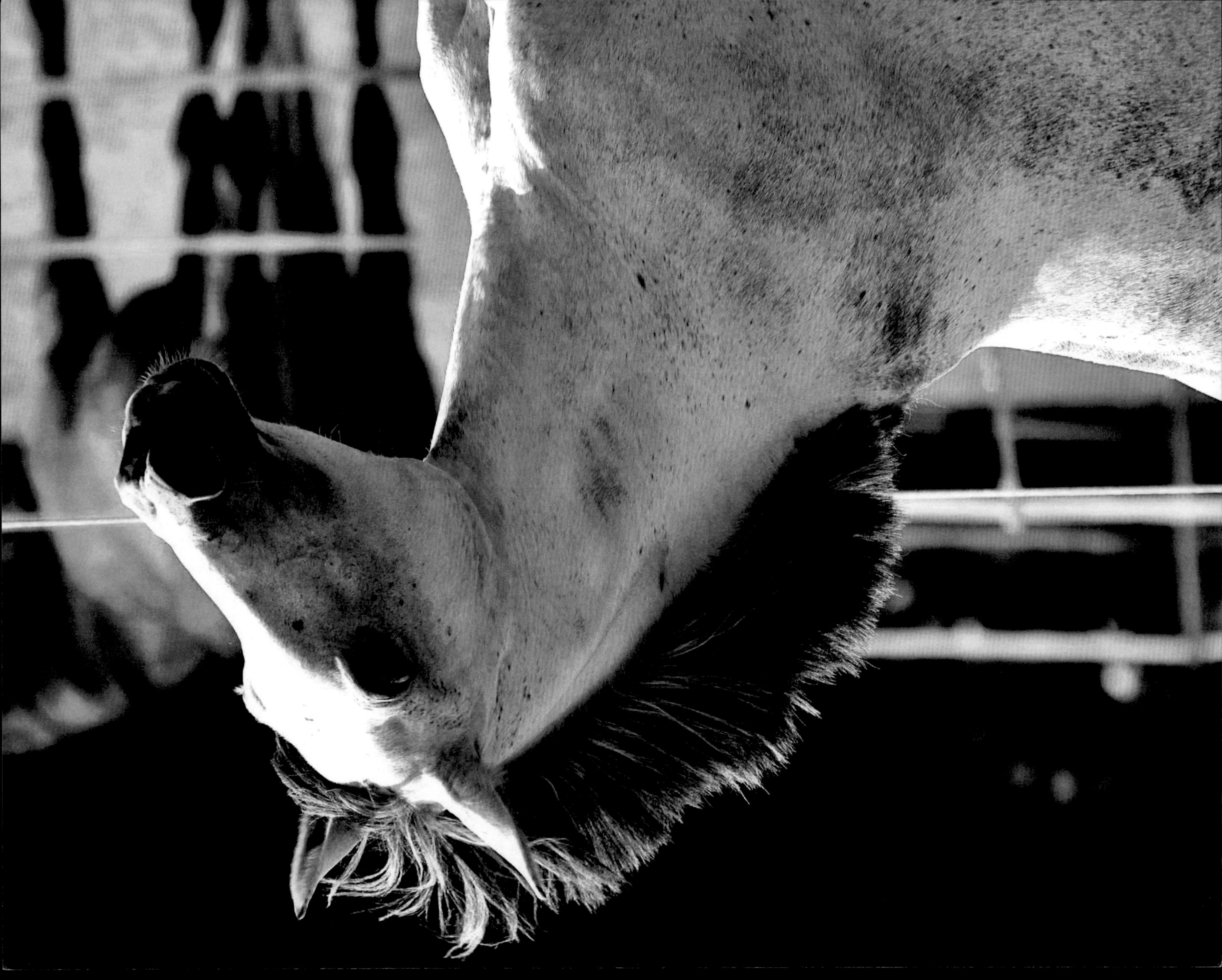

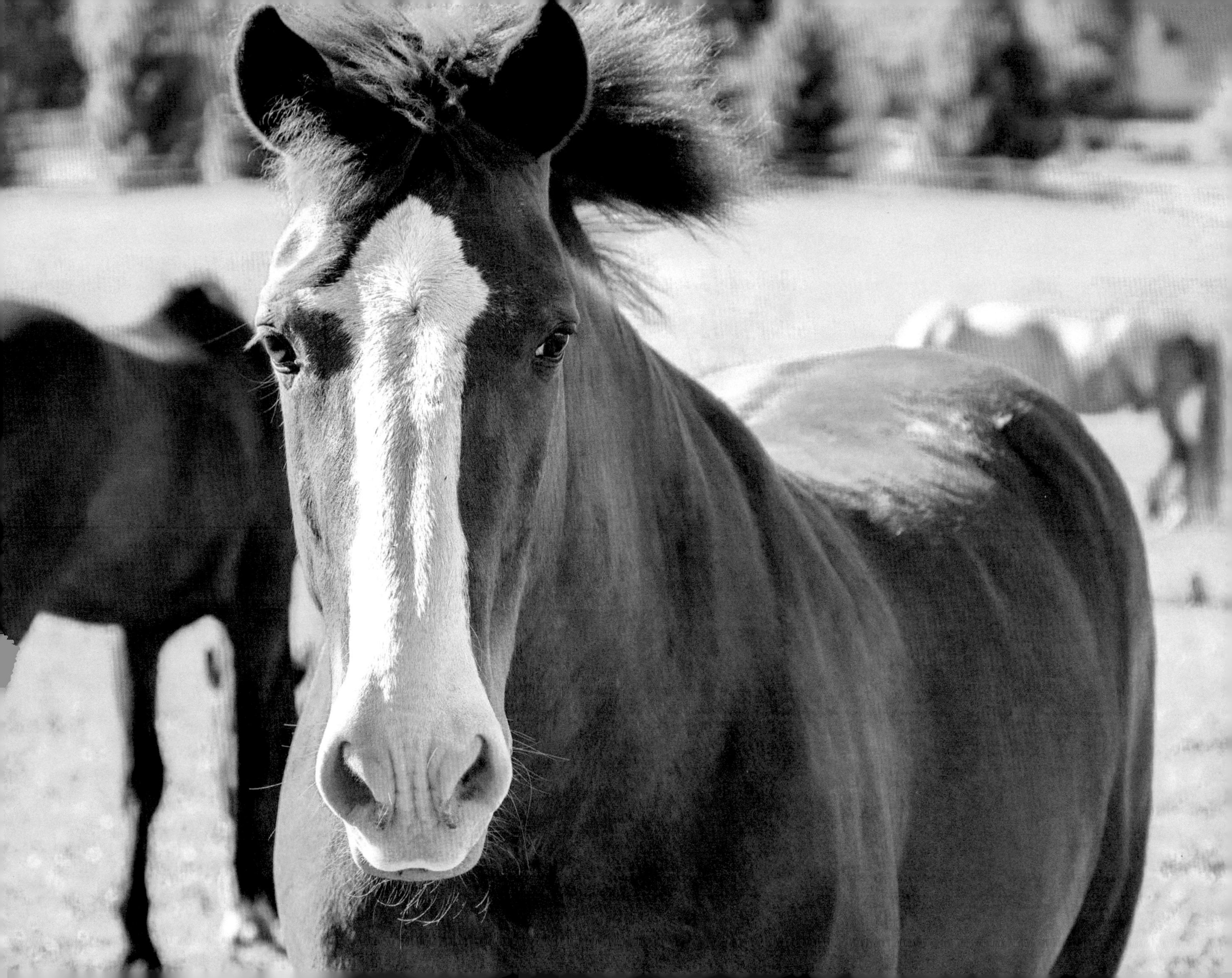

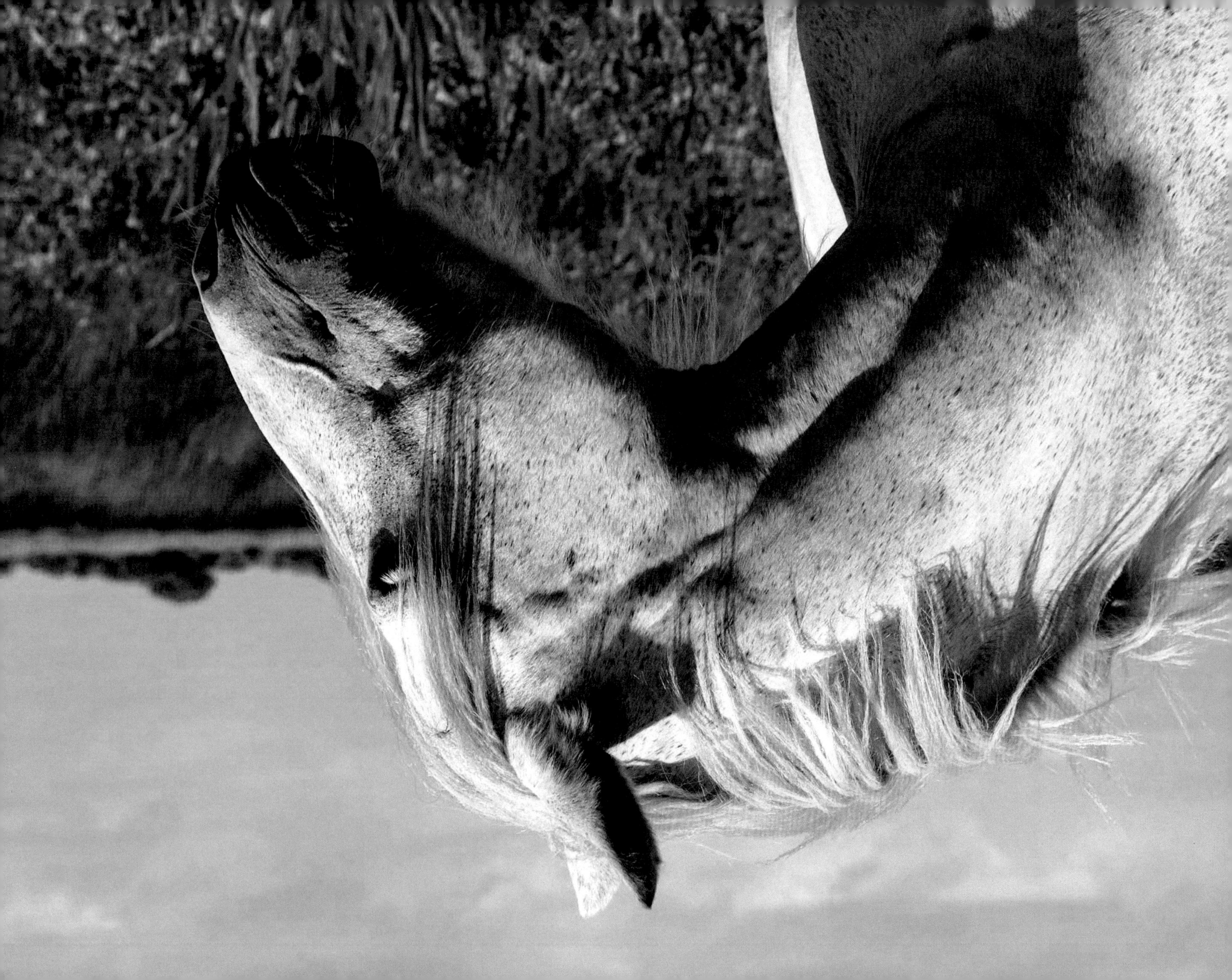

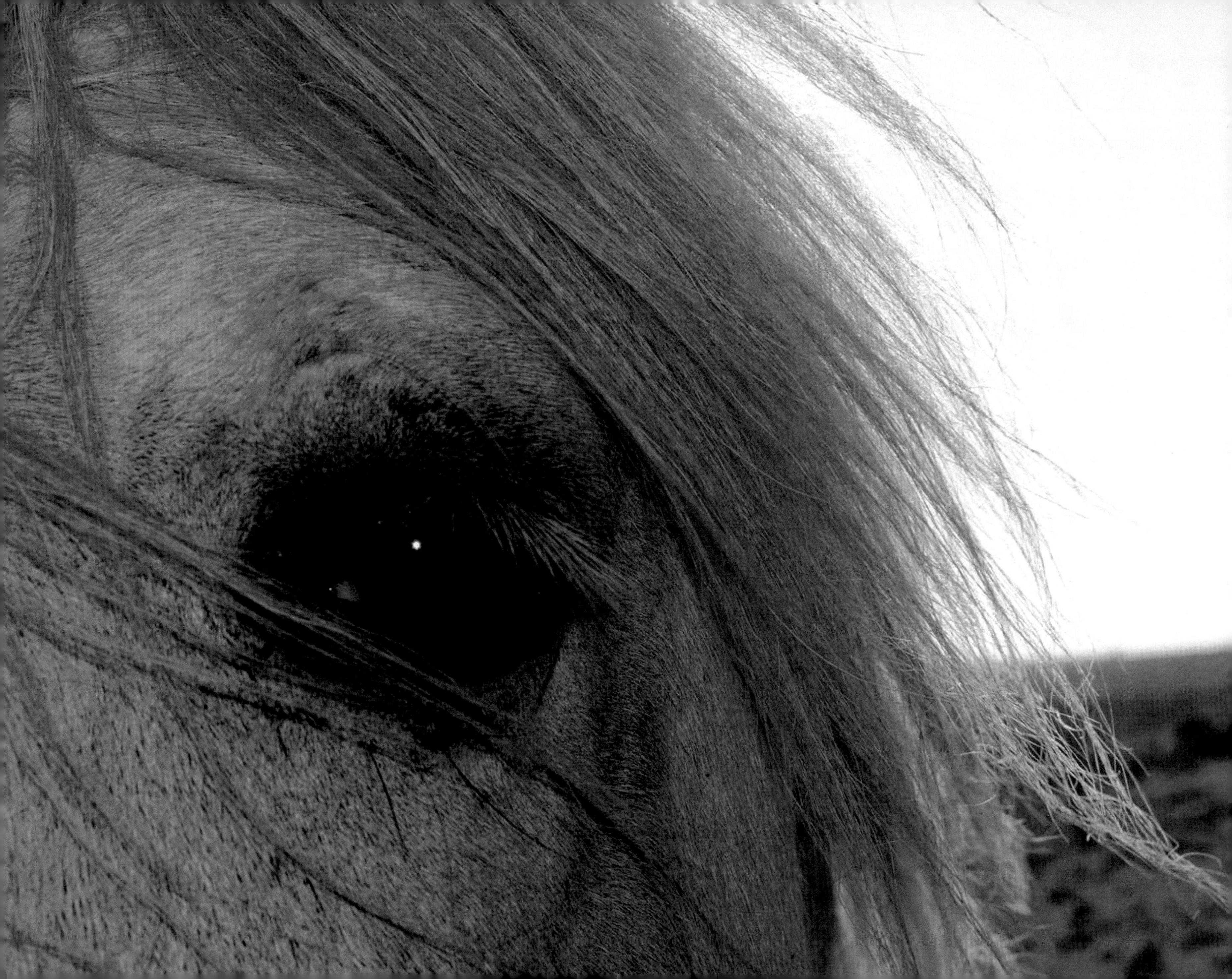

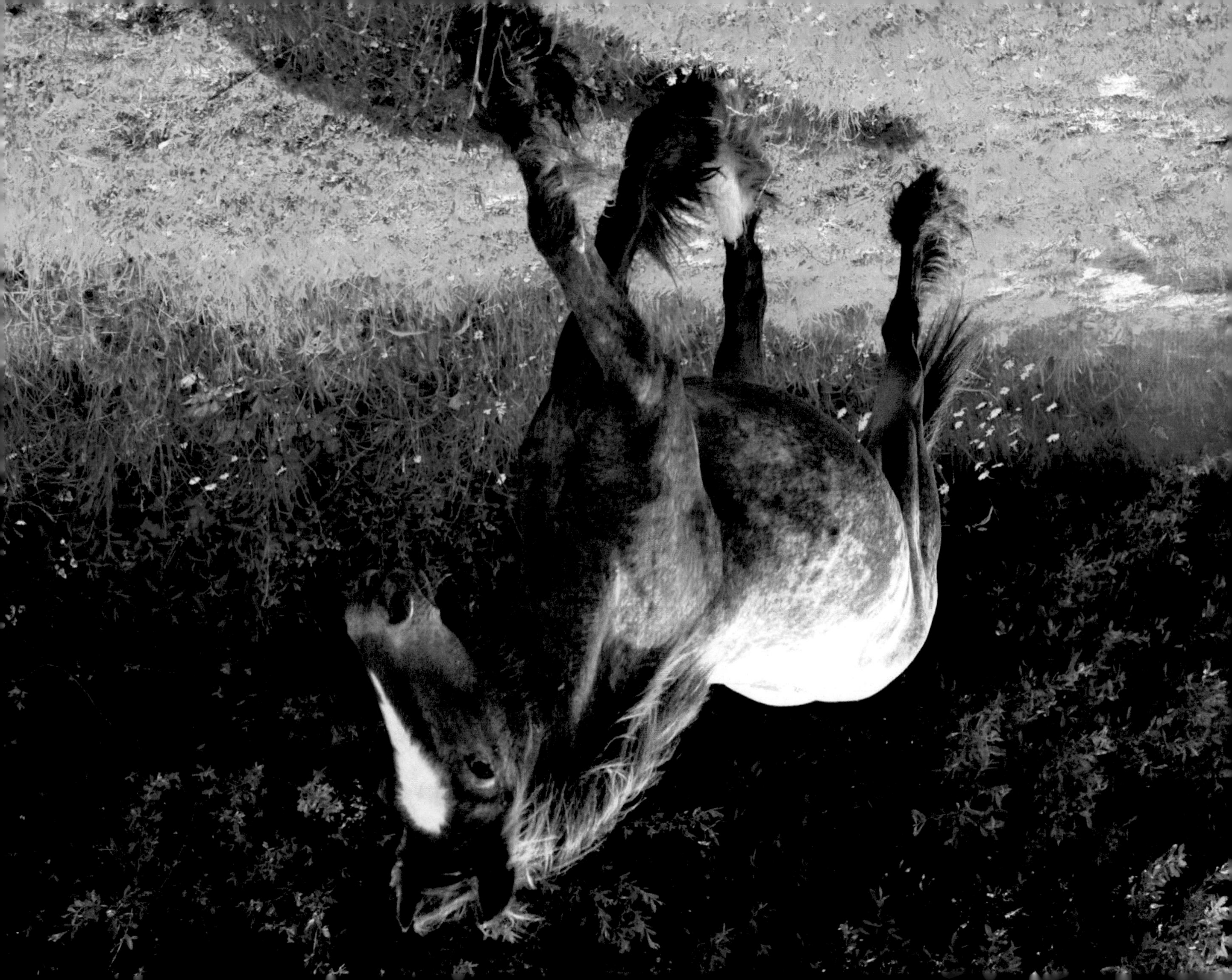

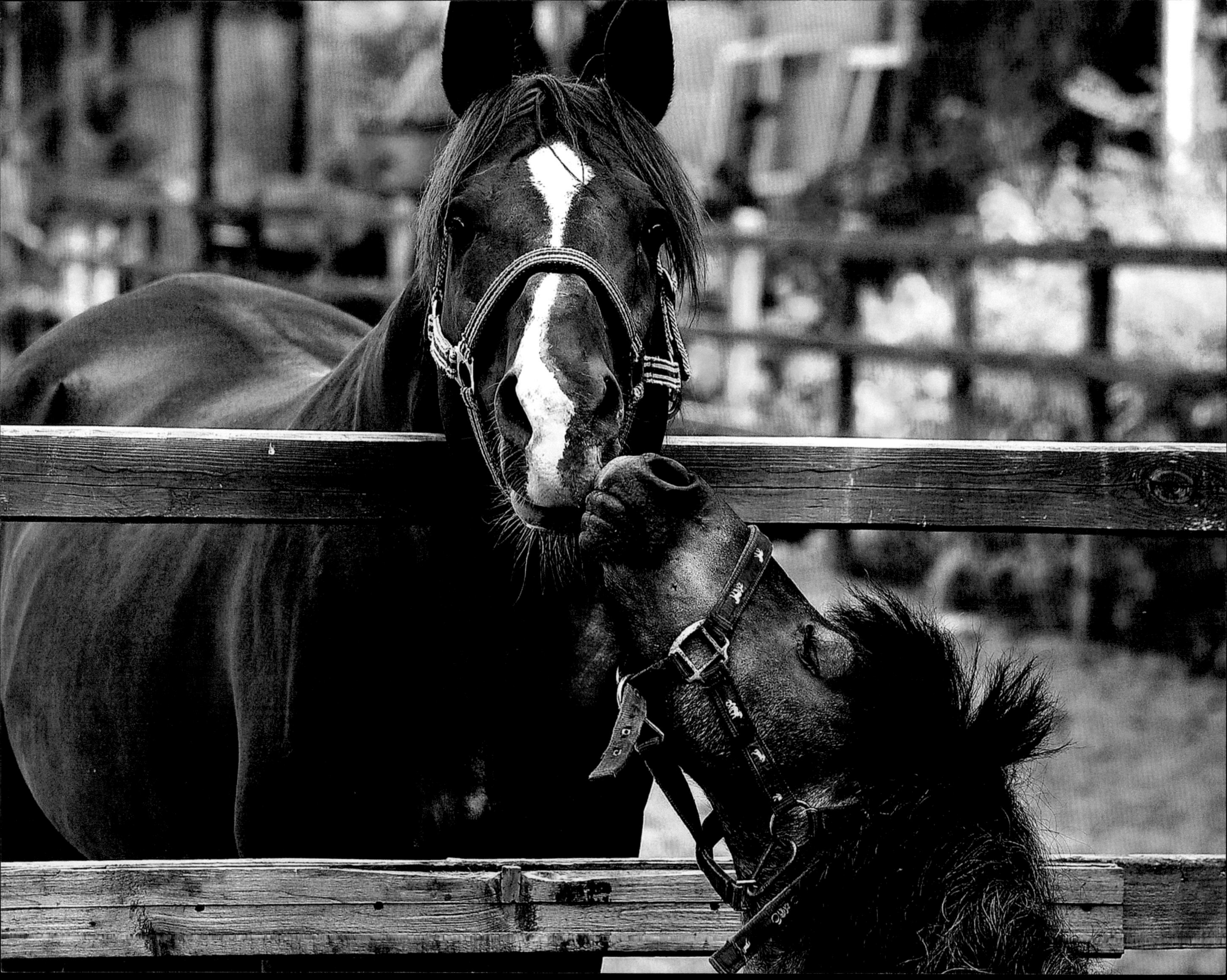

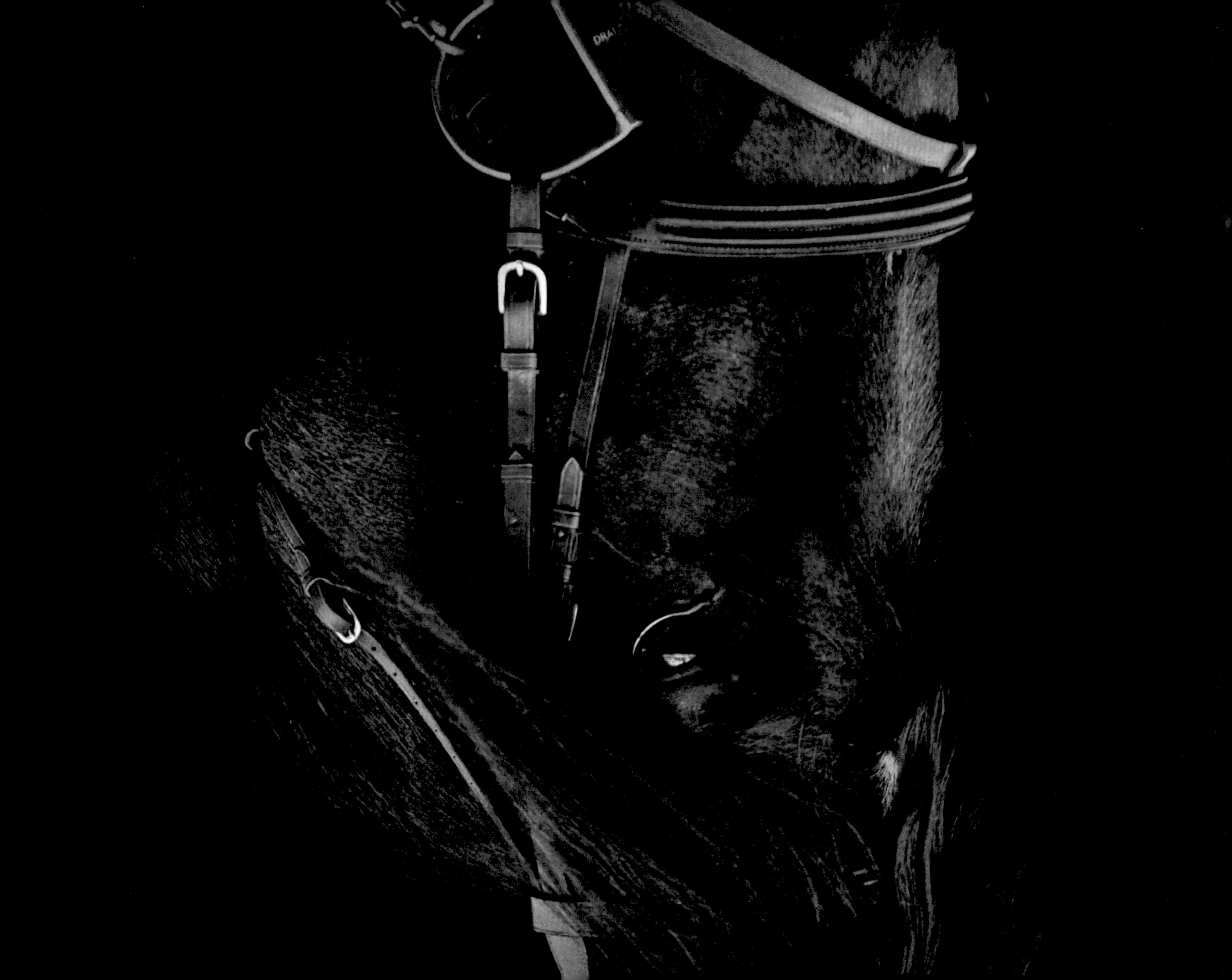

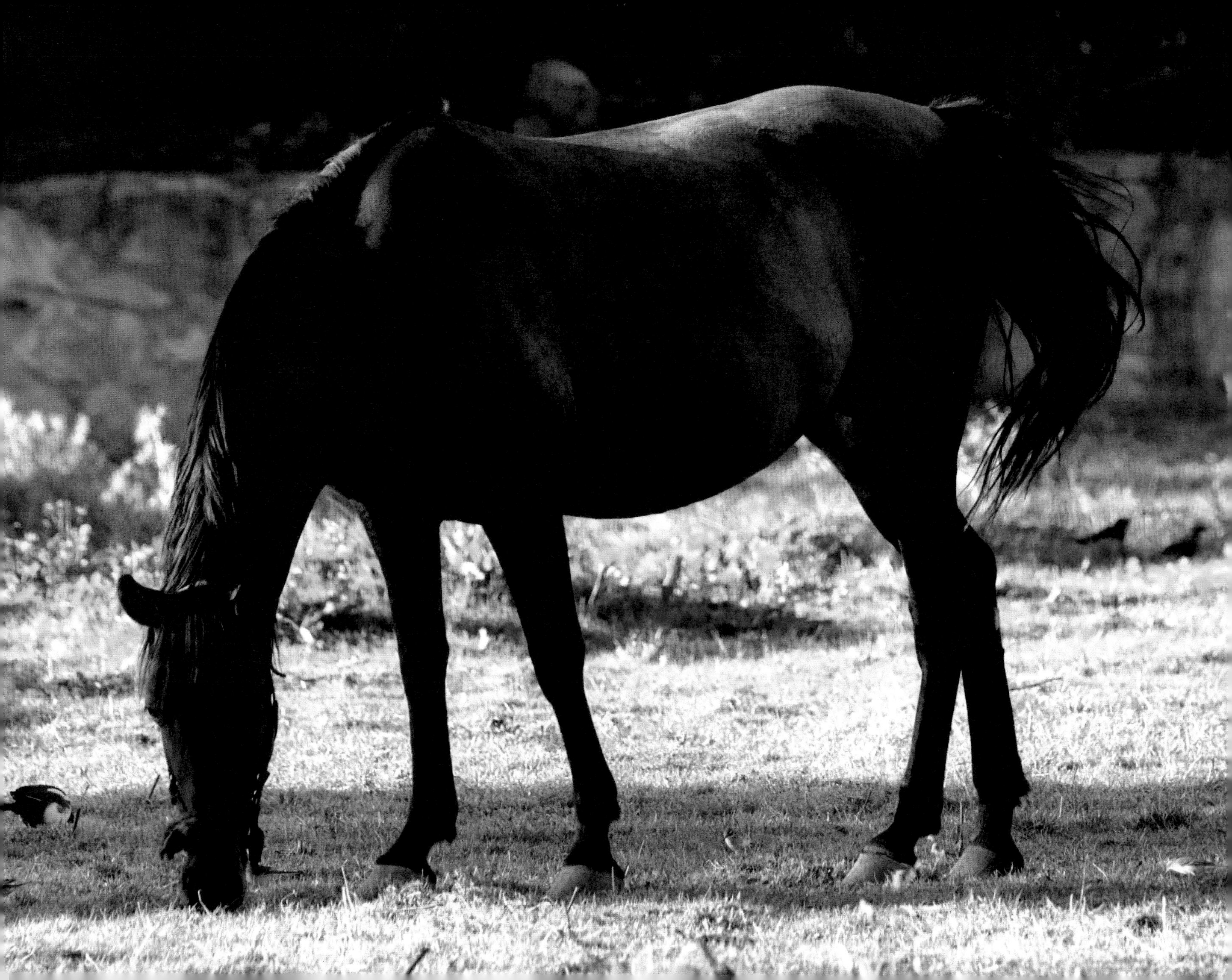

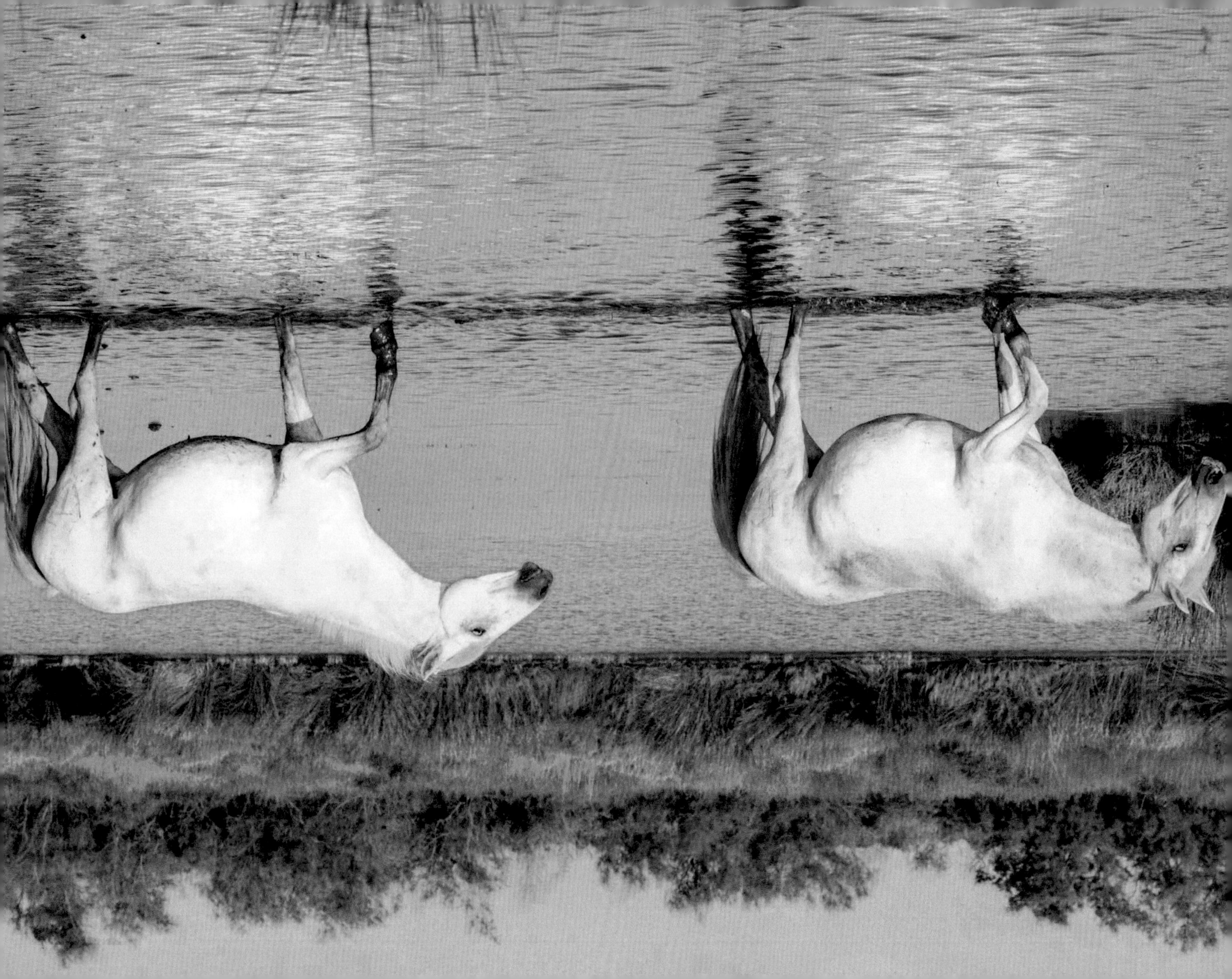

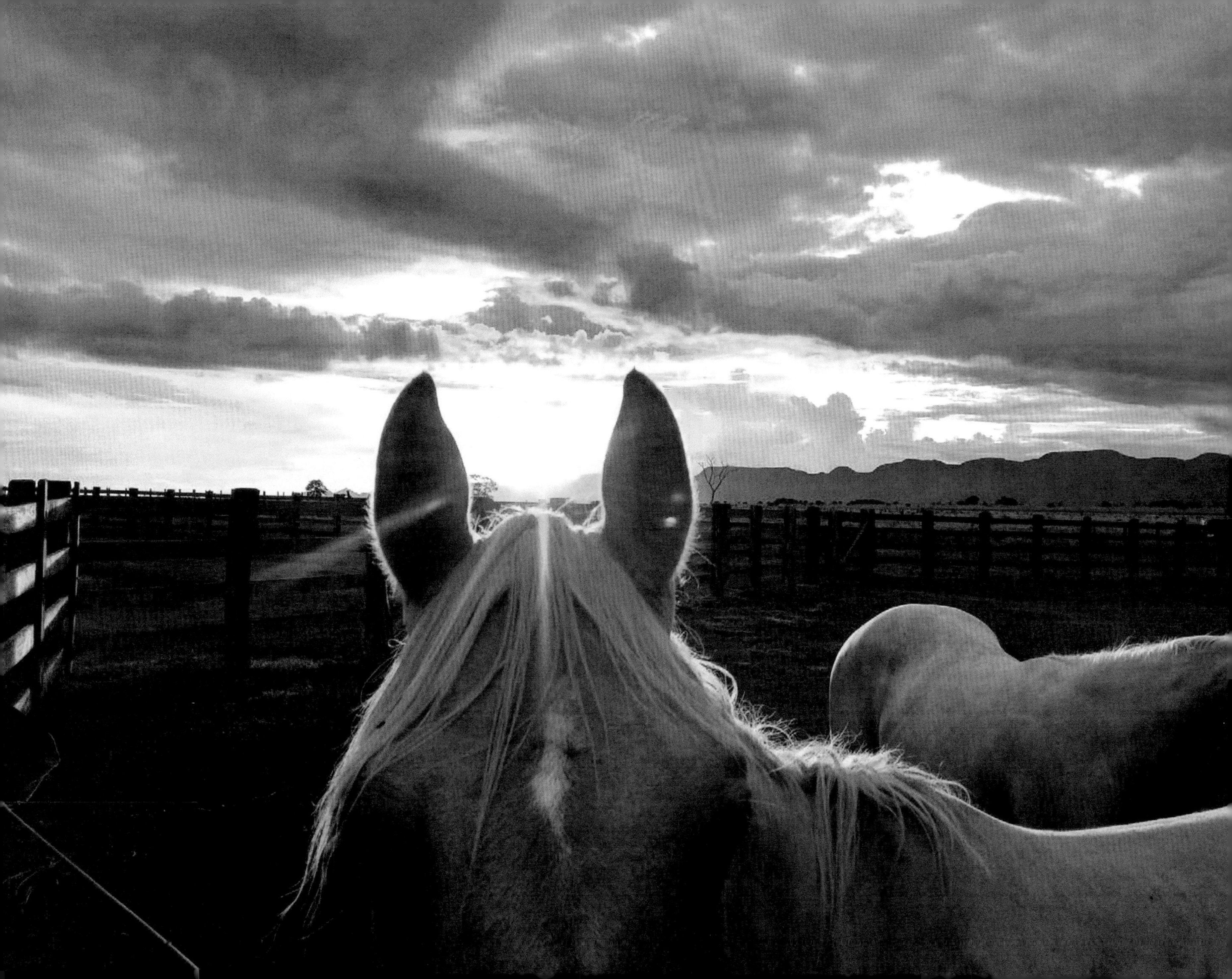

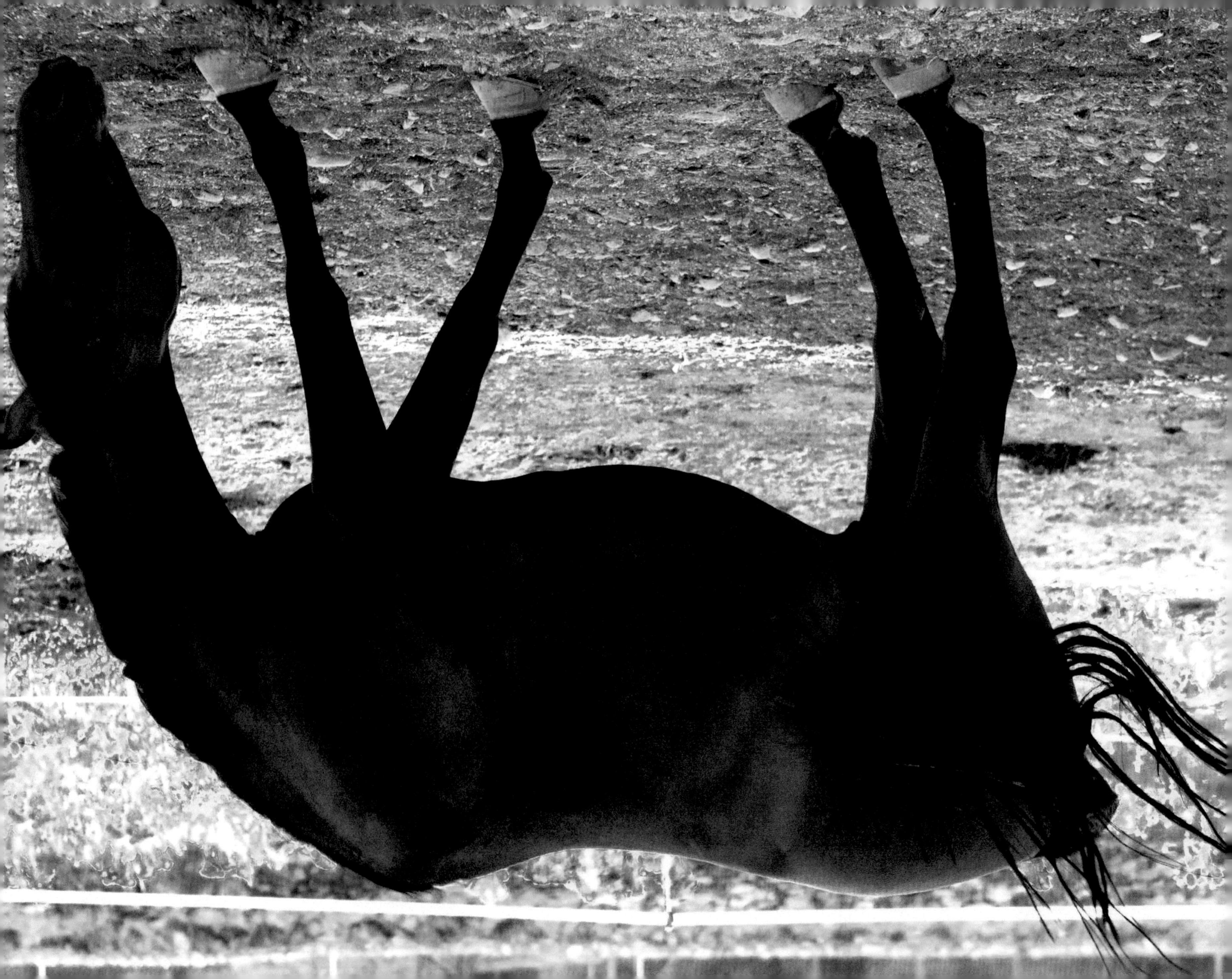

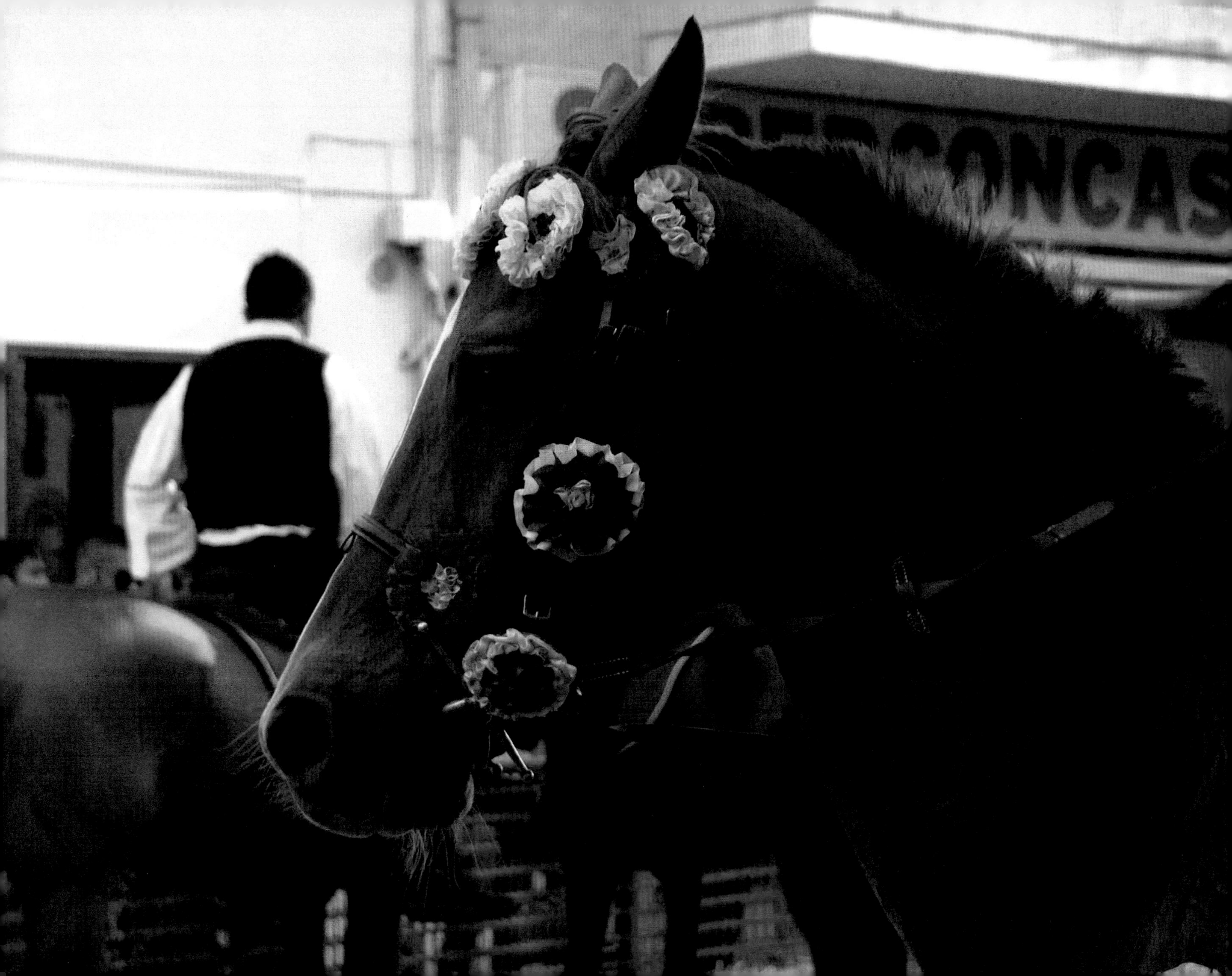
CONCAS

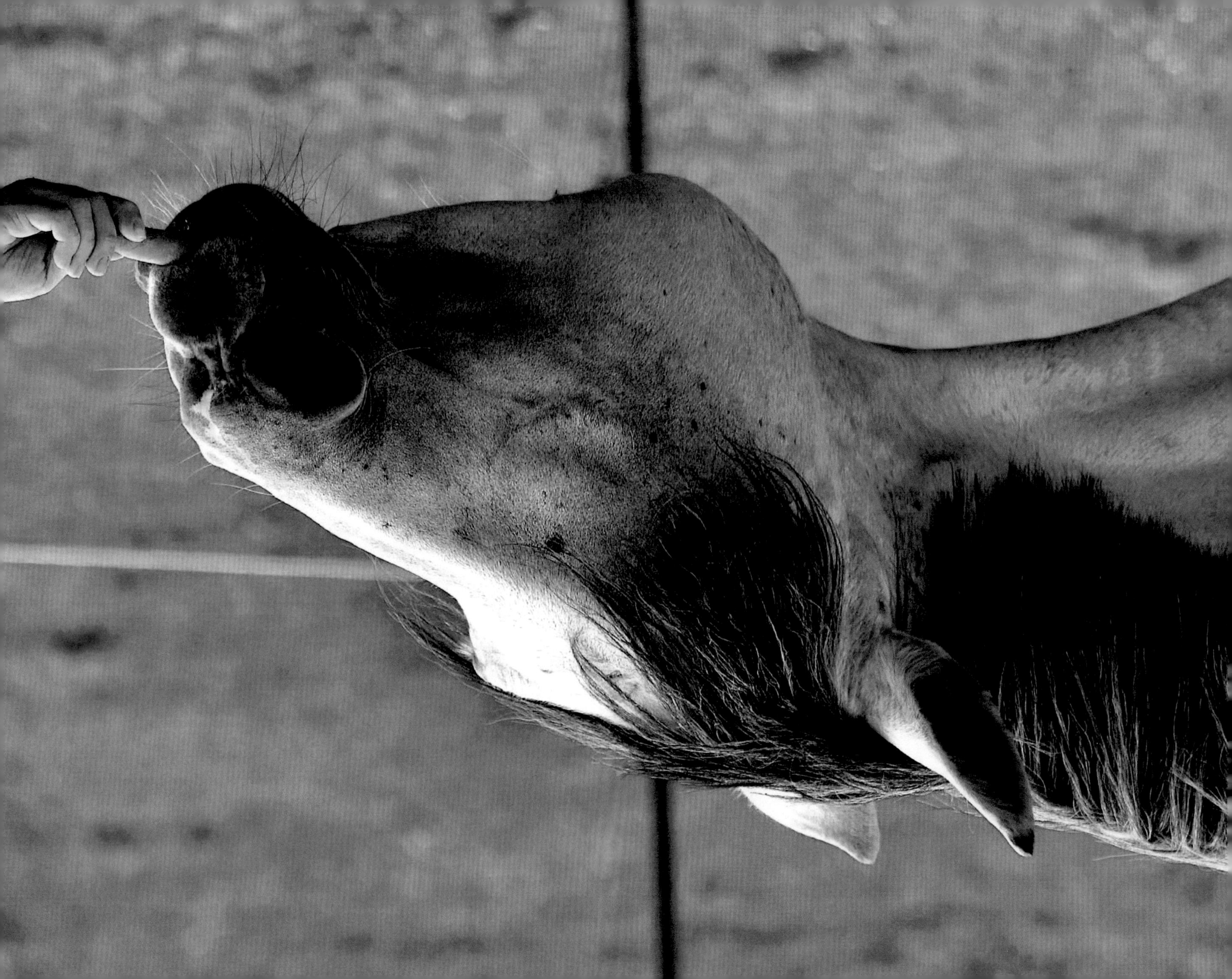

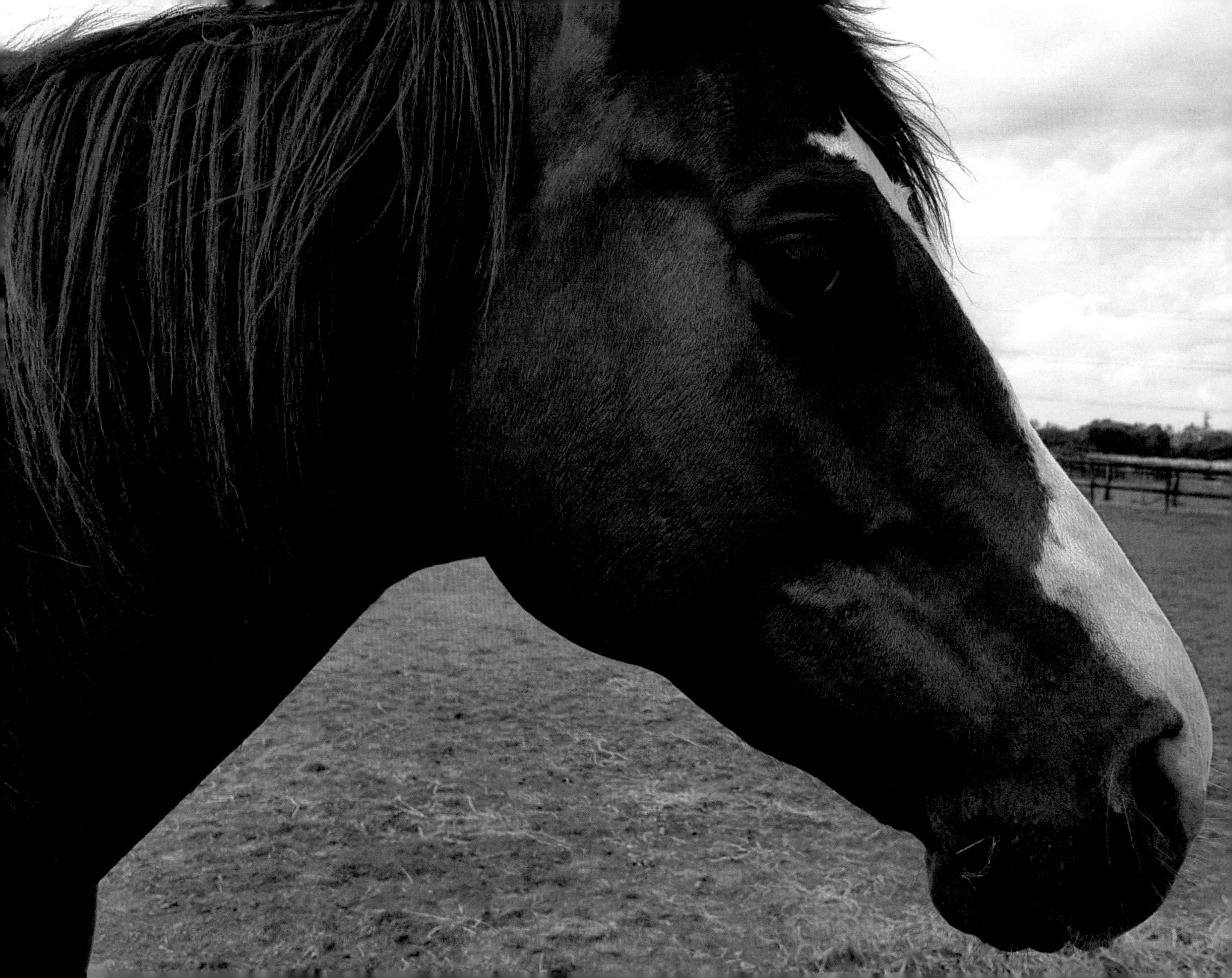

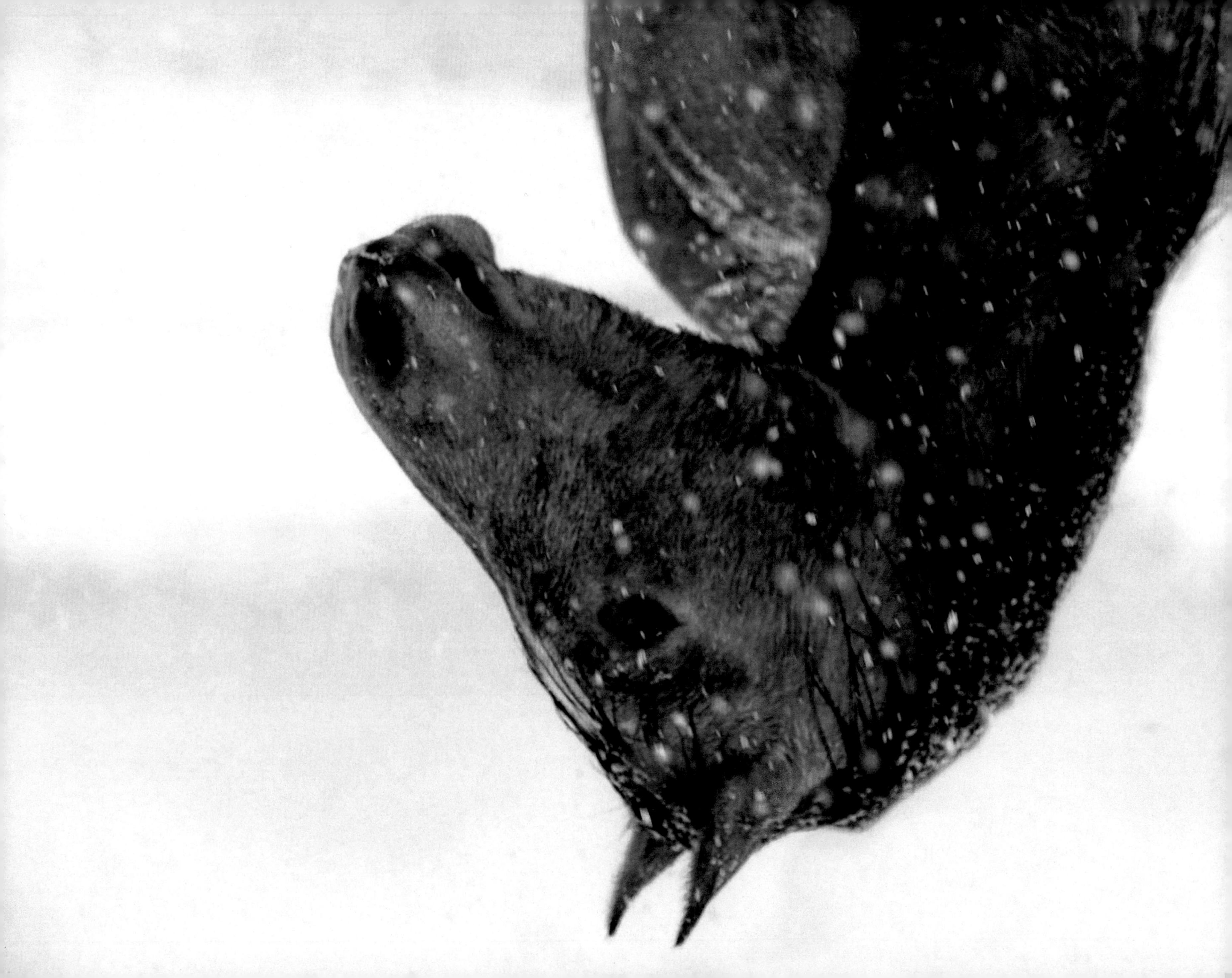

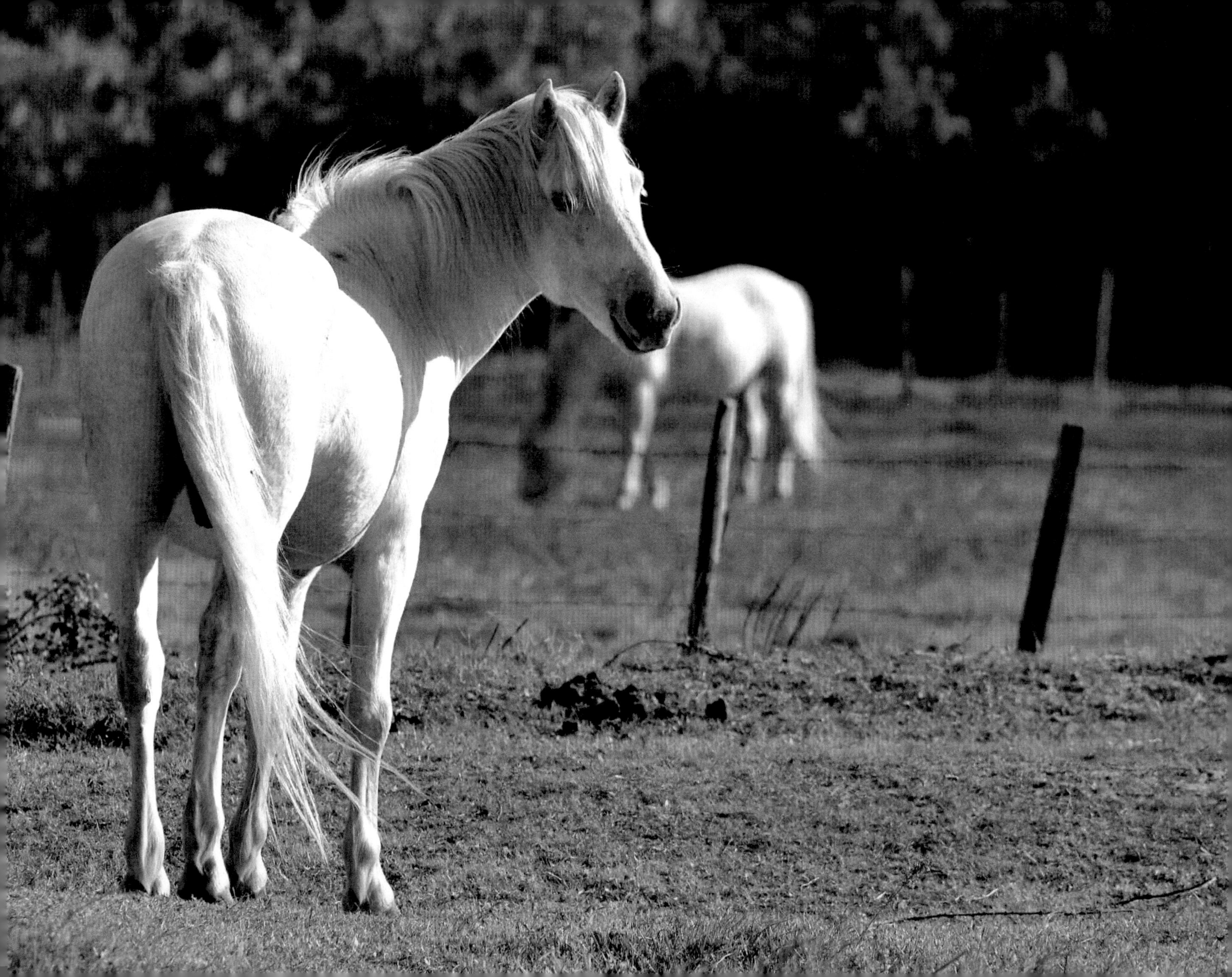

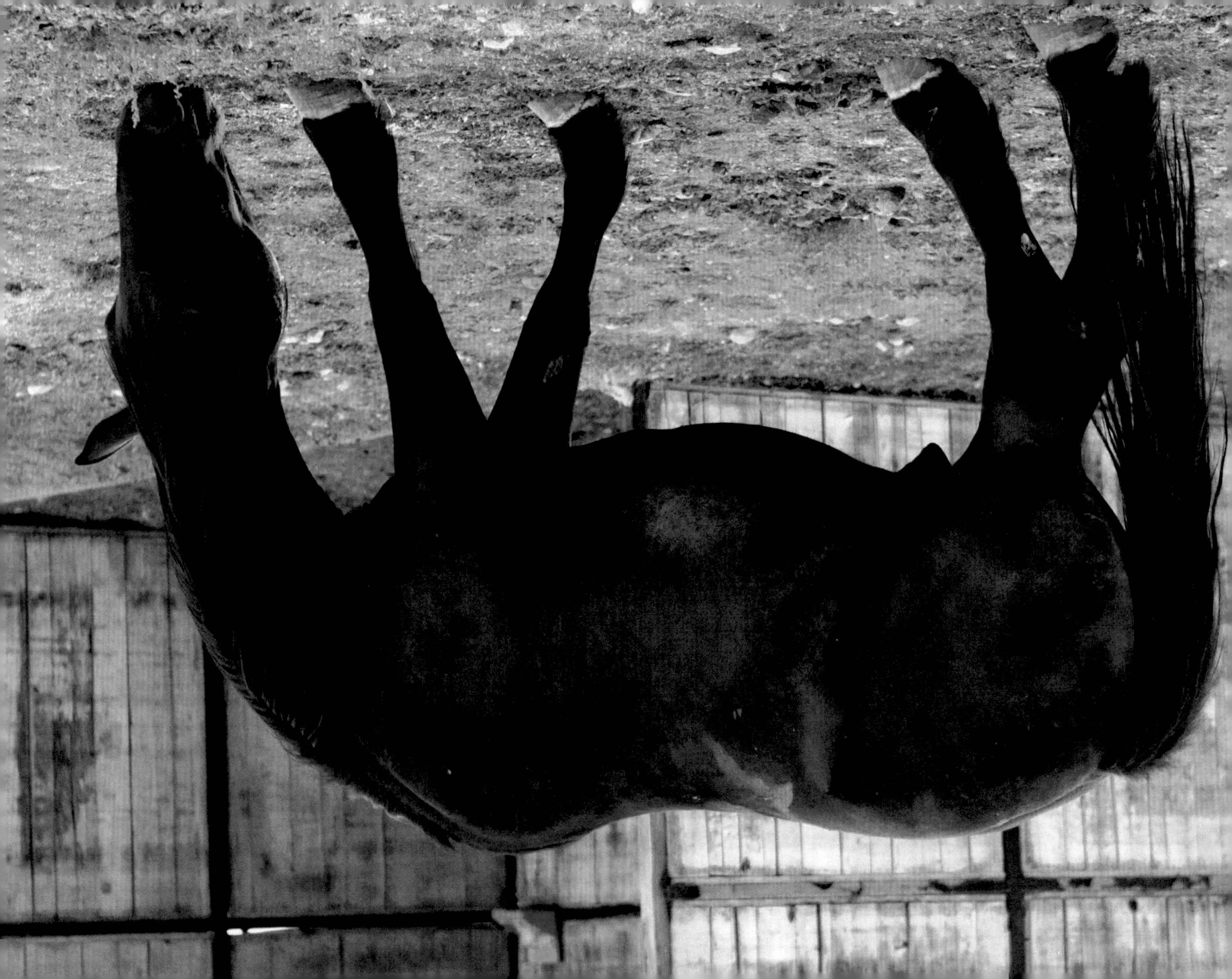

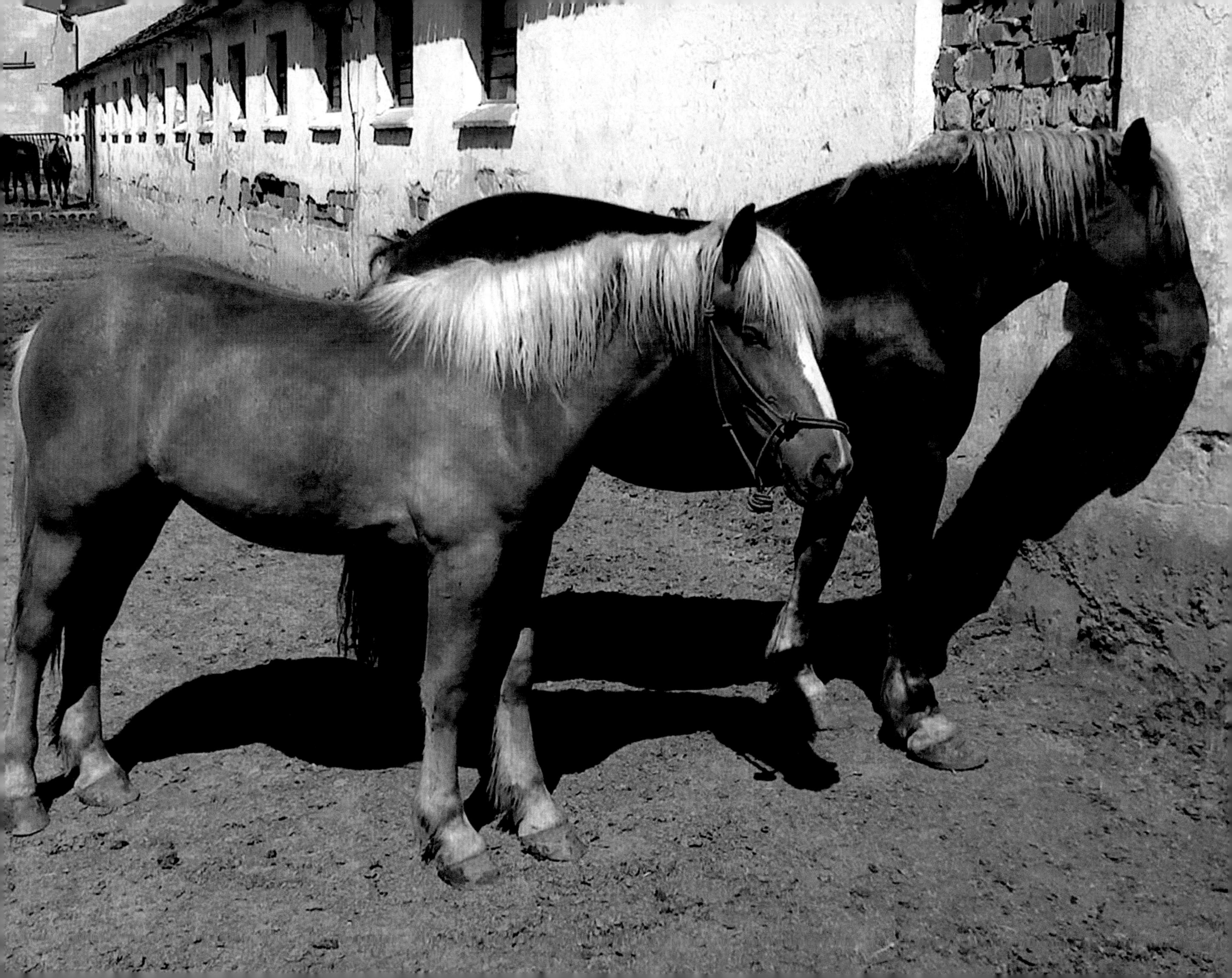

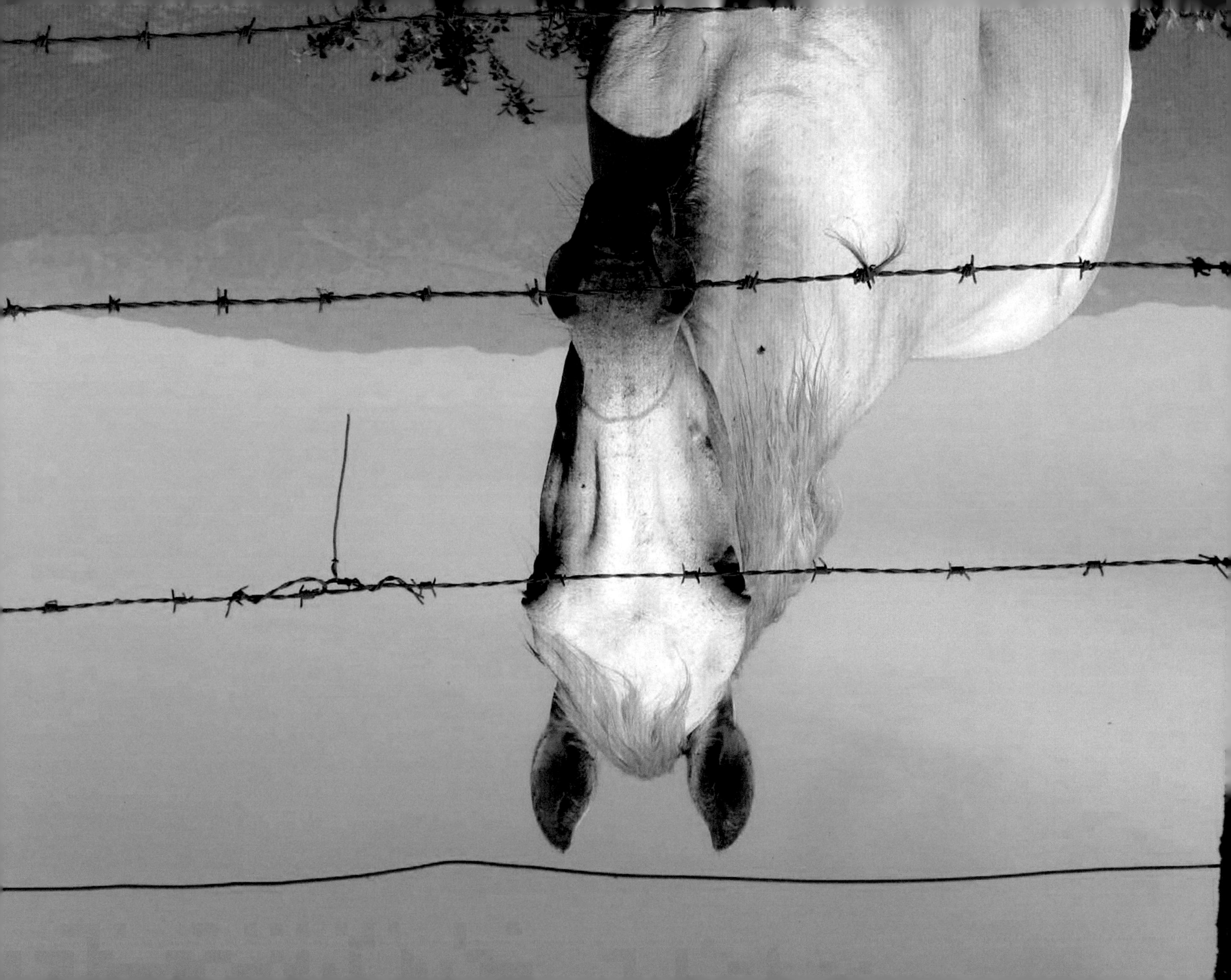

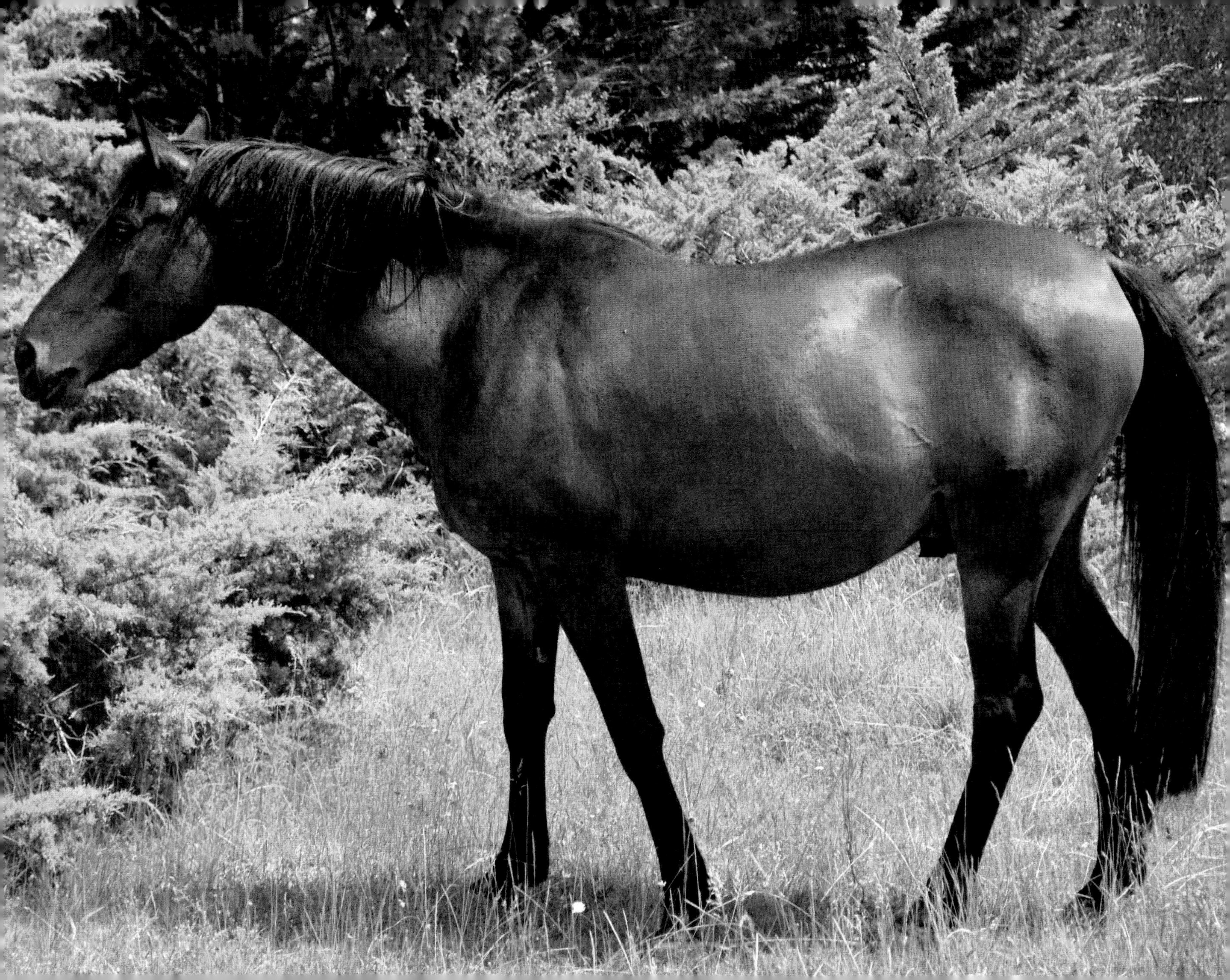

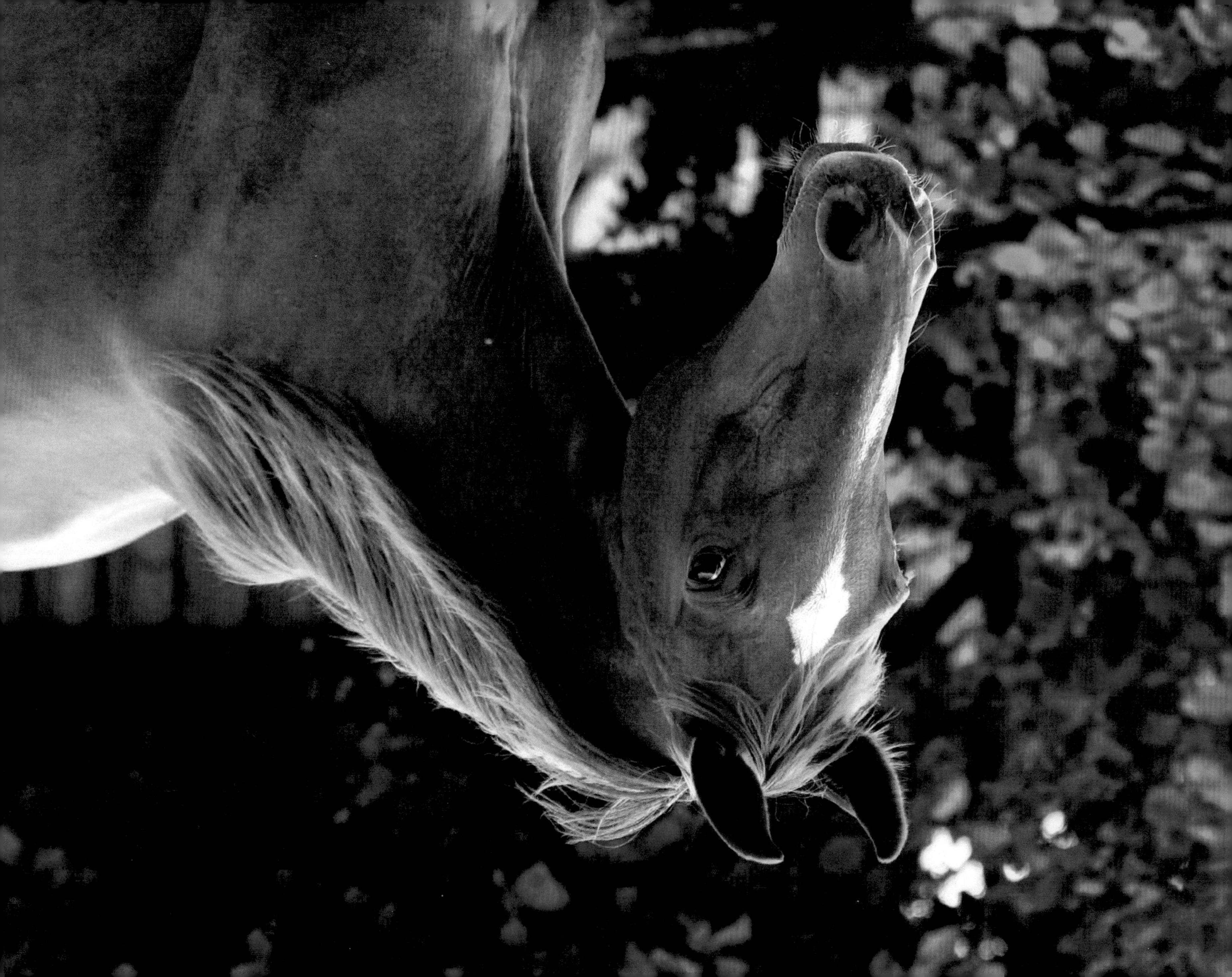

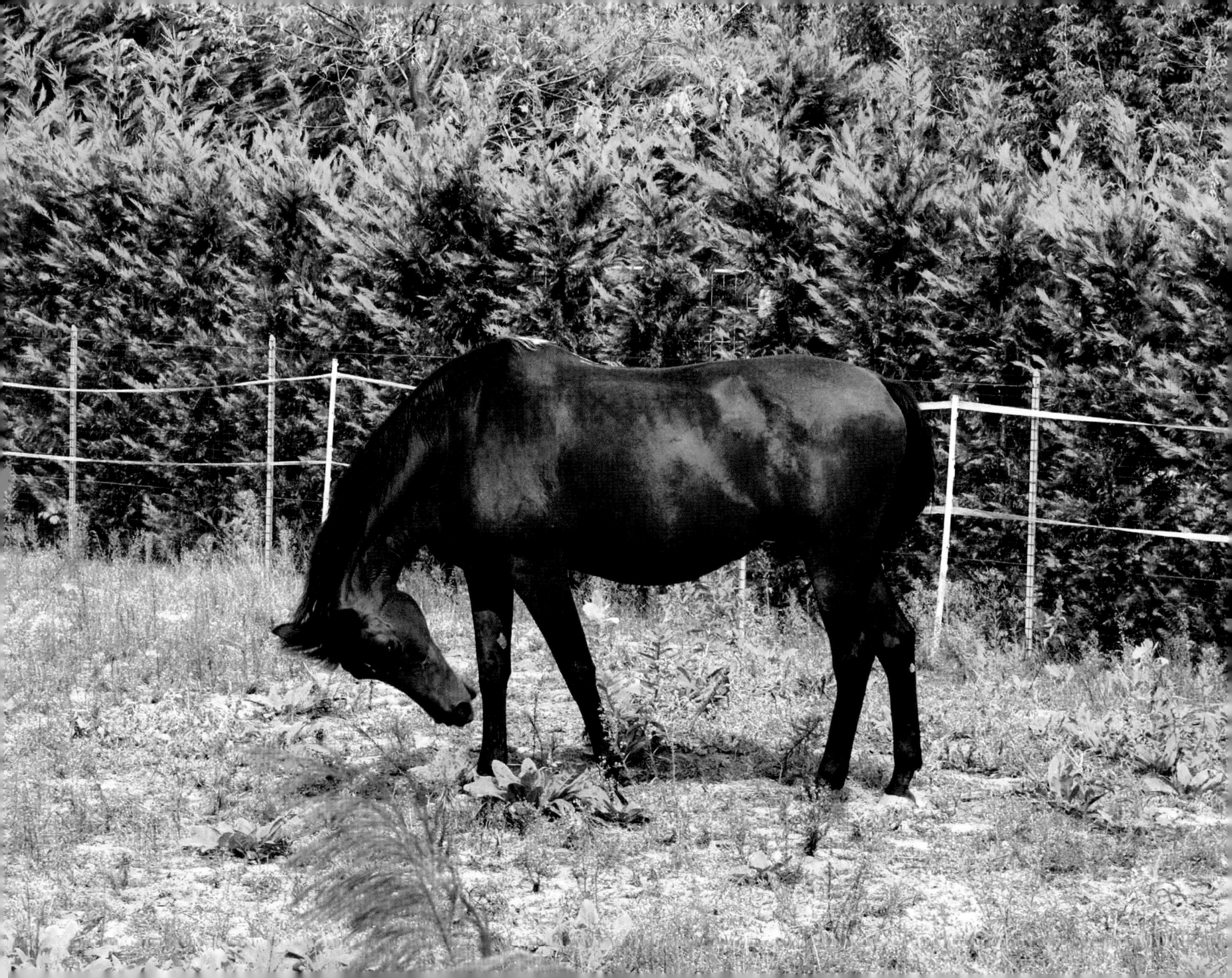

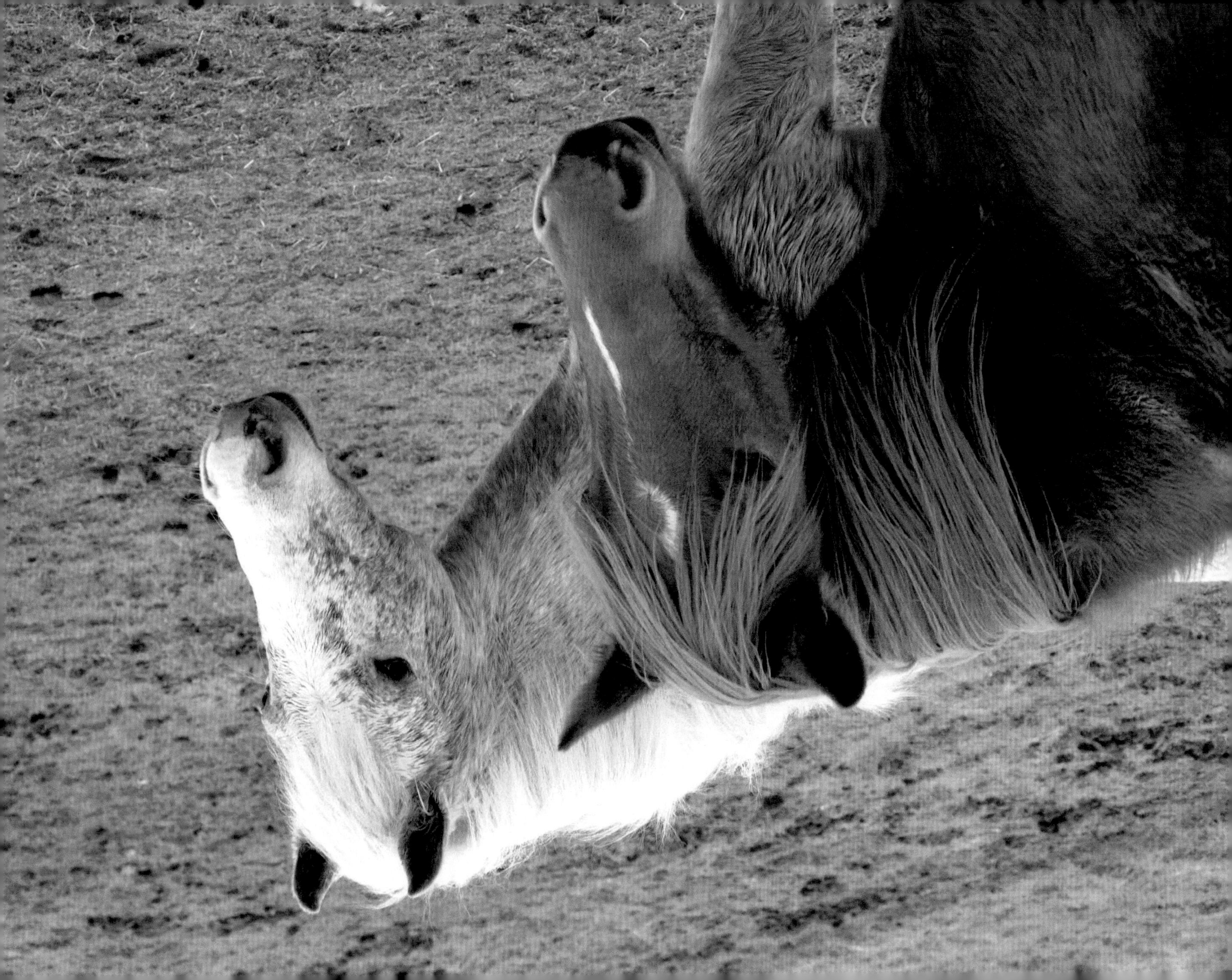

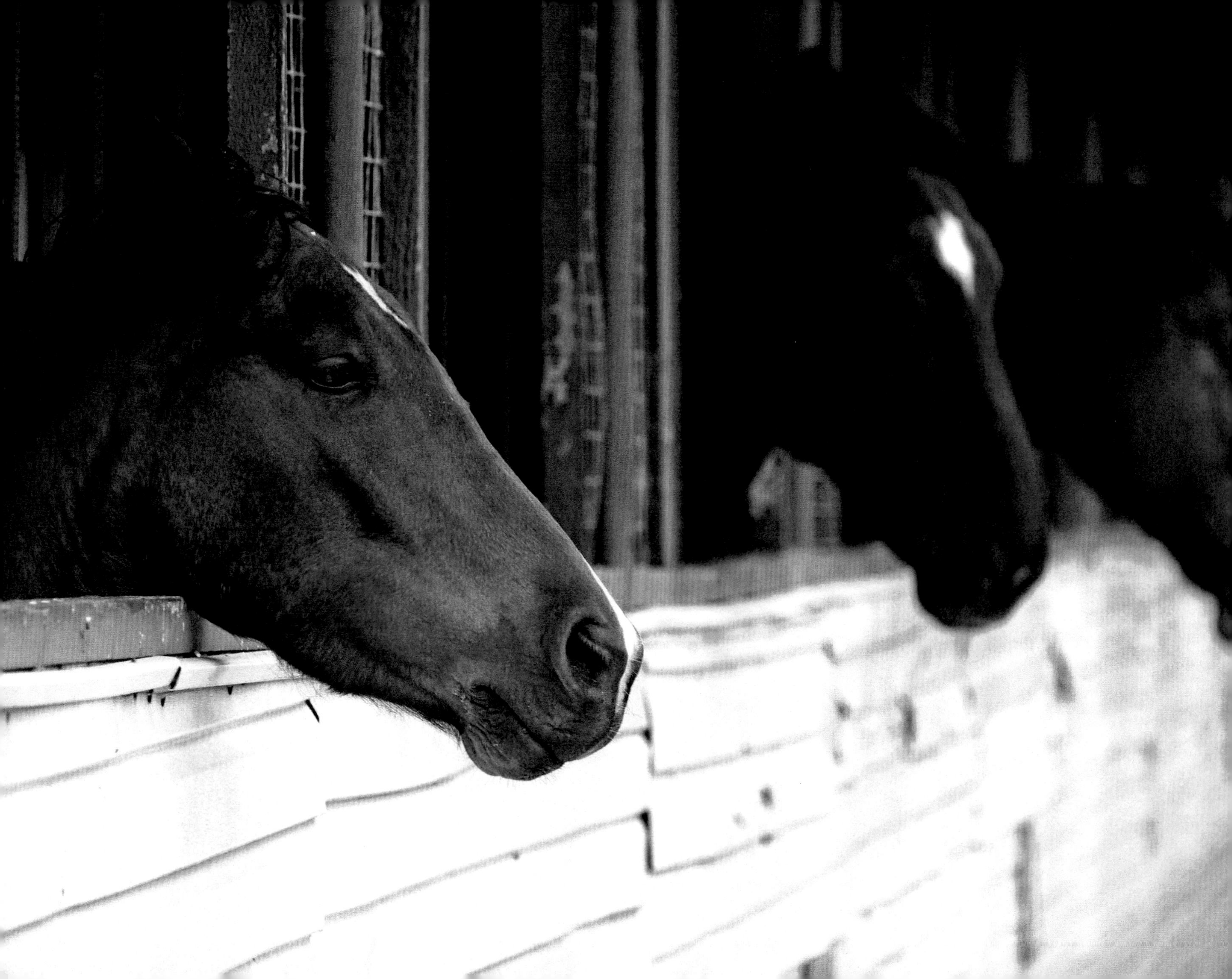

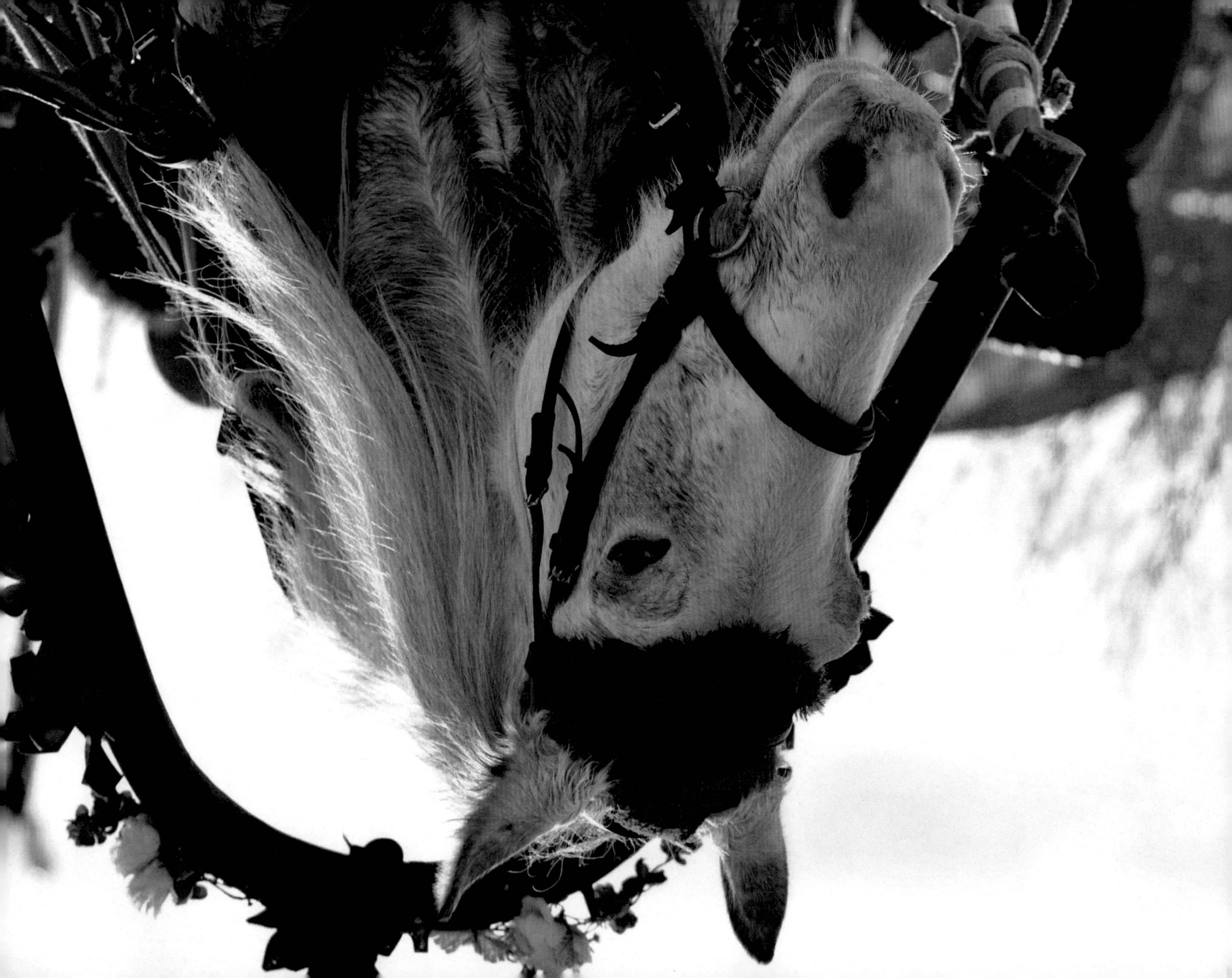

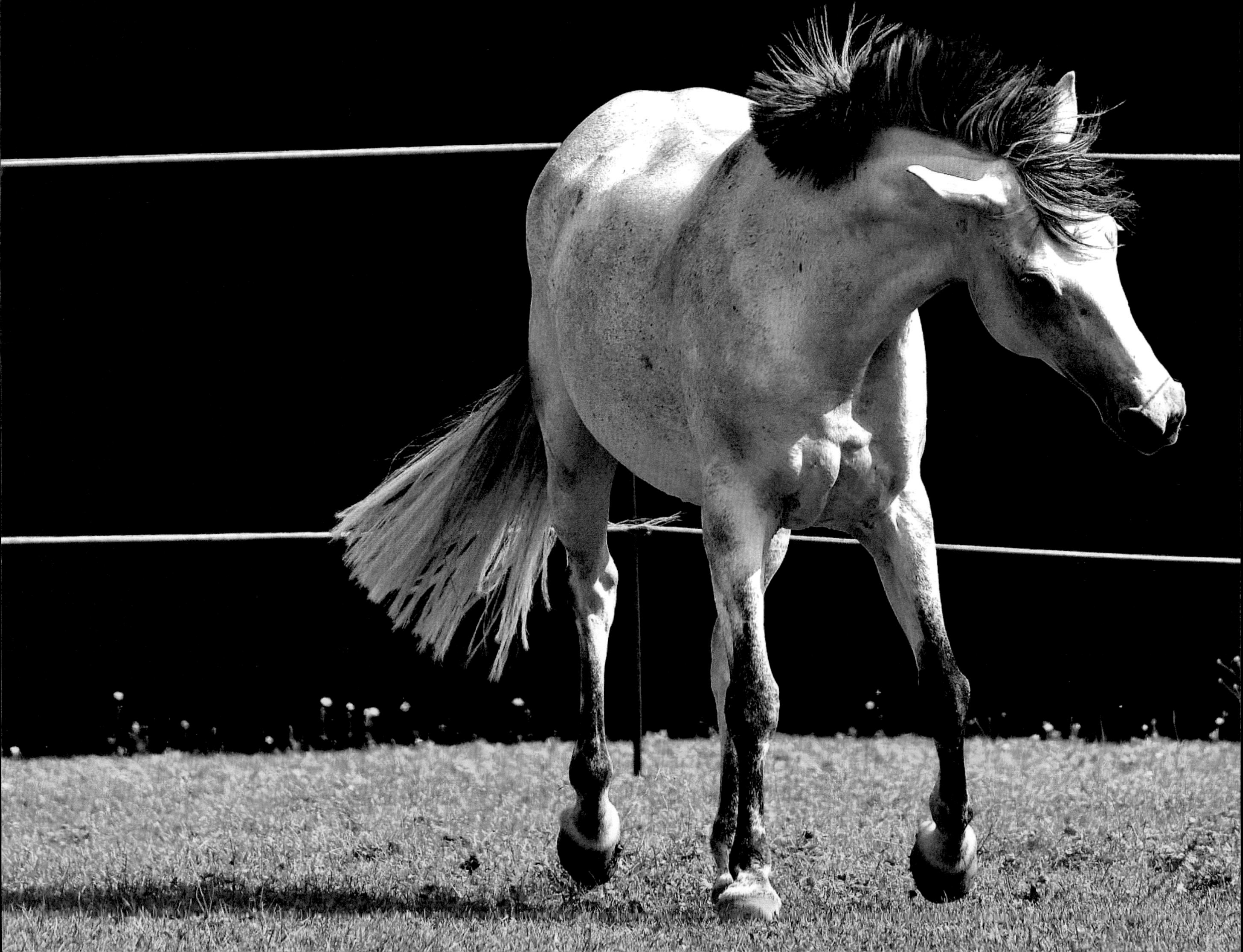

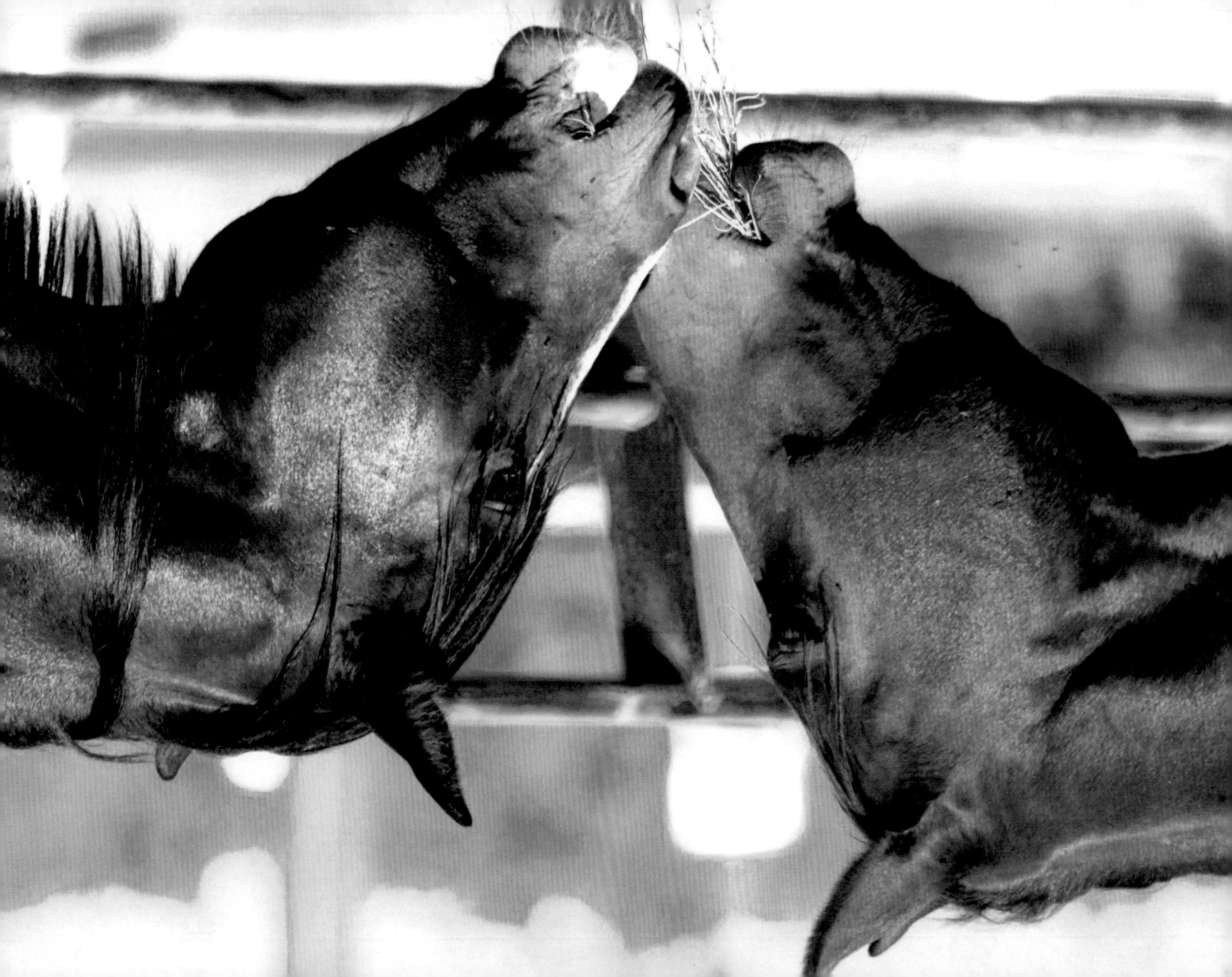

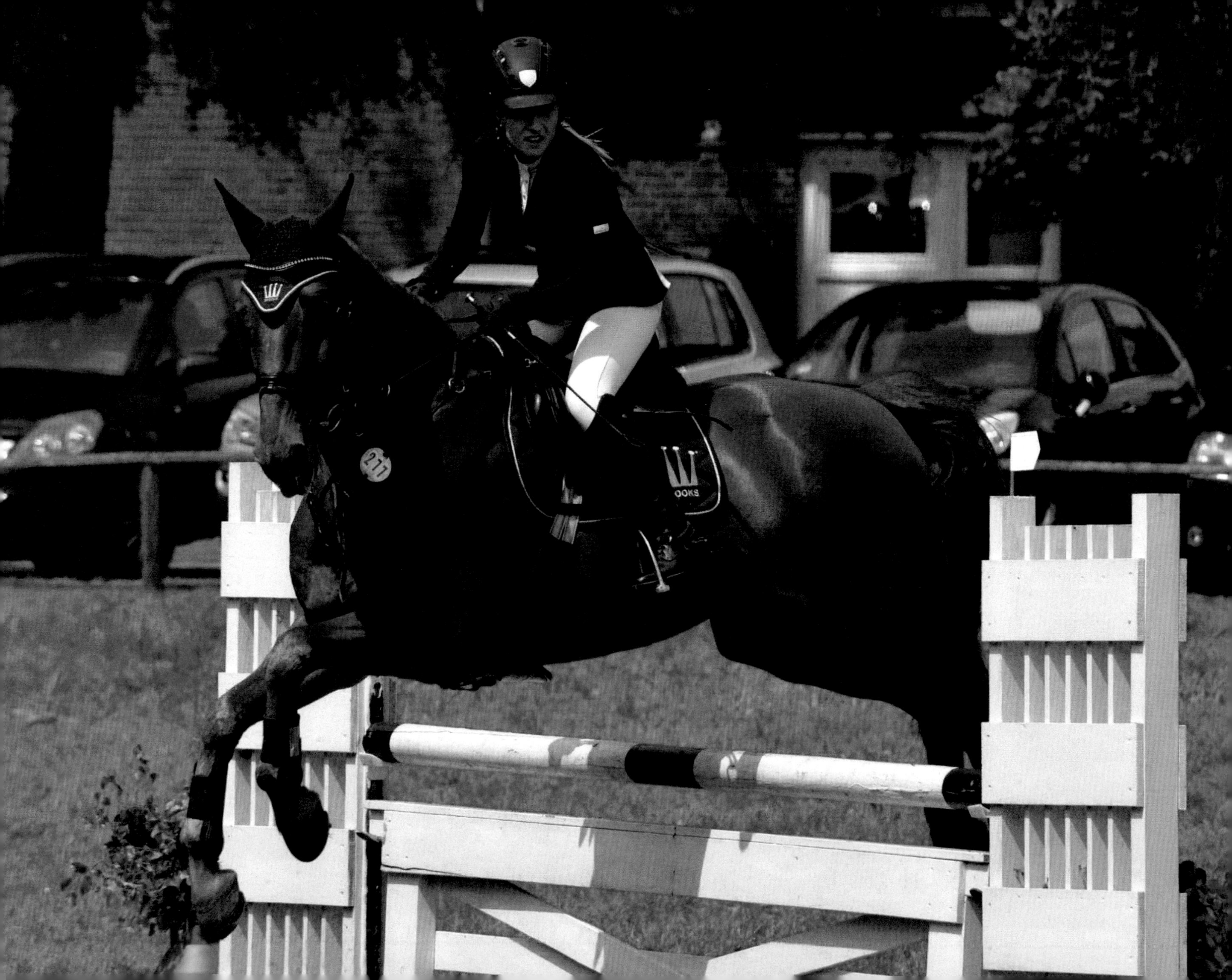
217

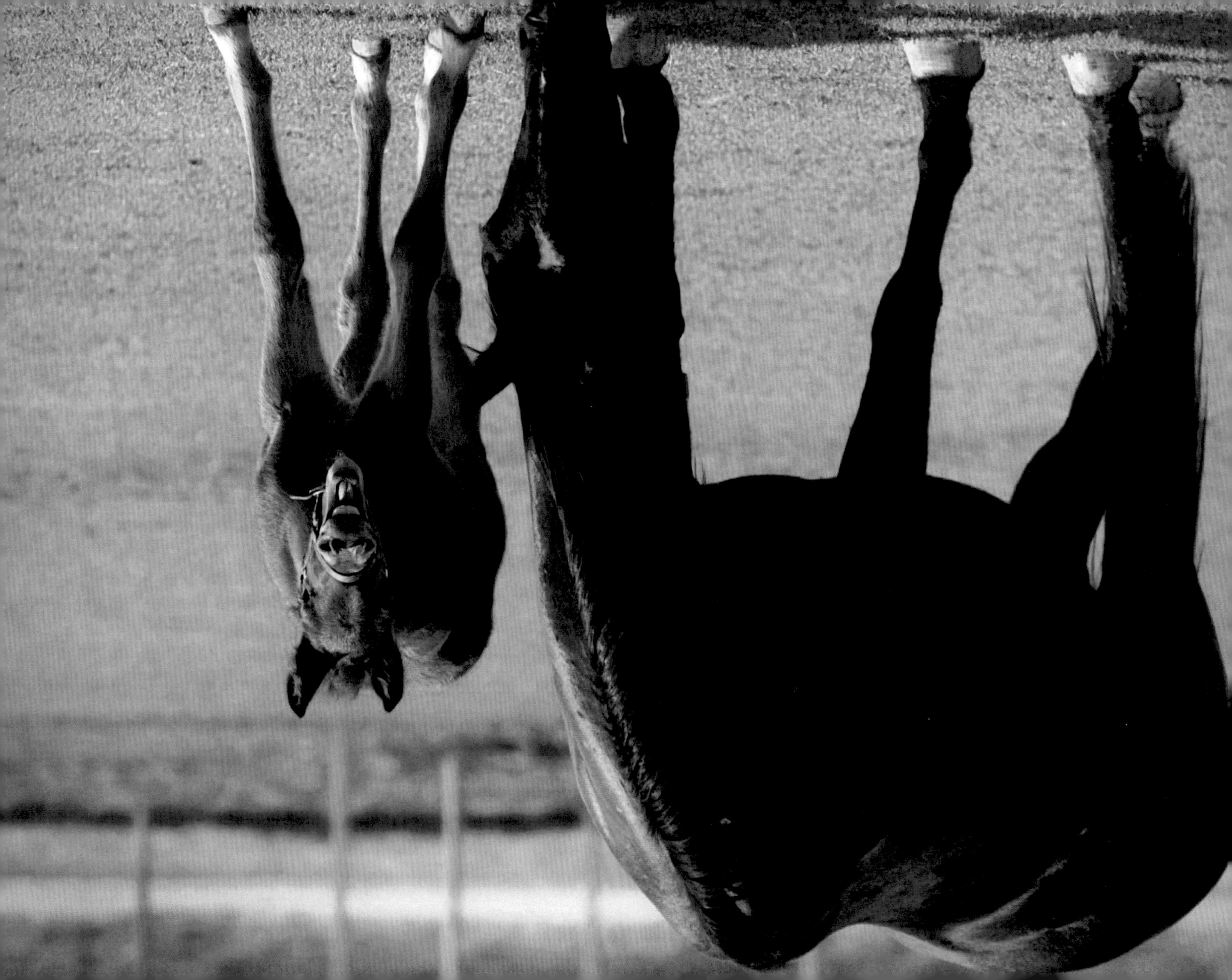

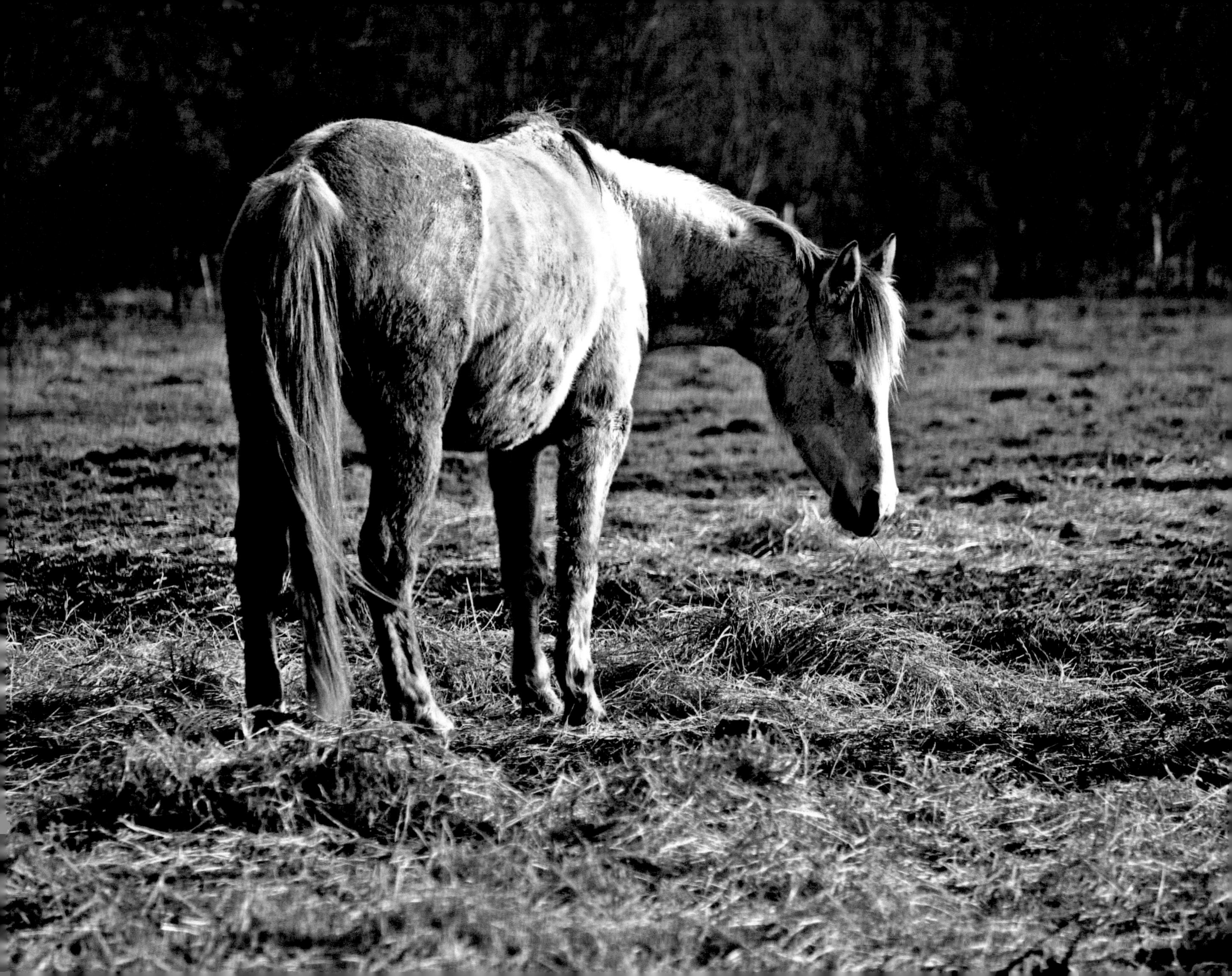

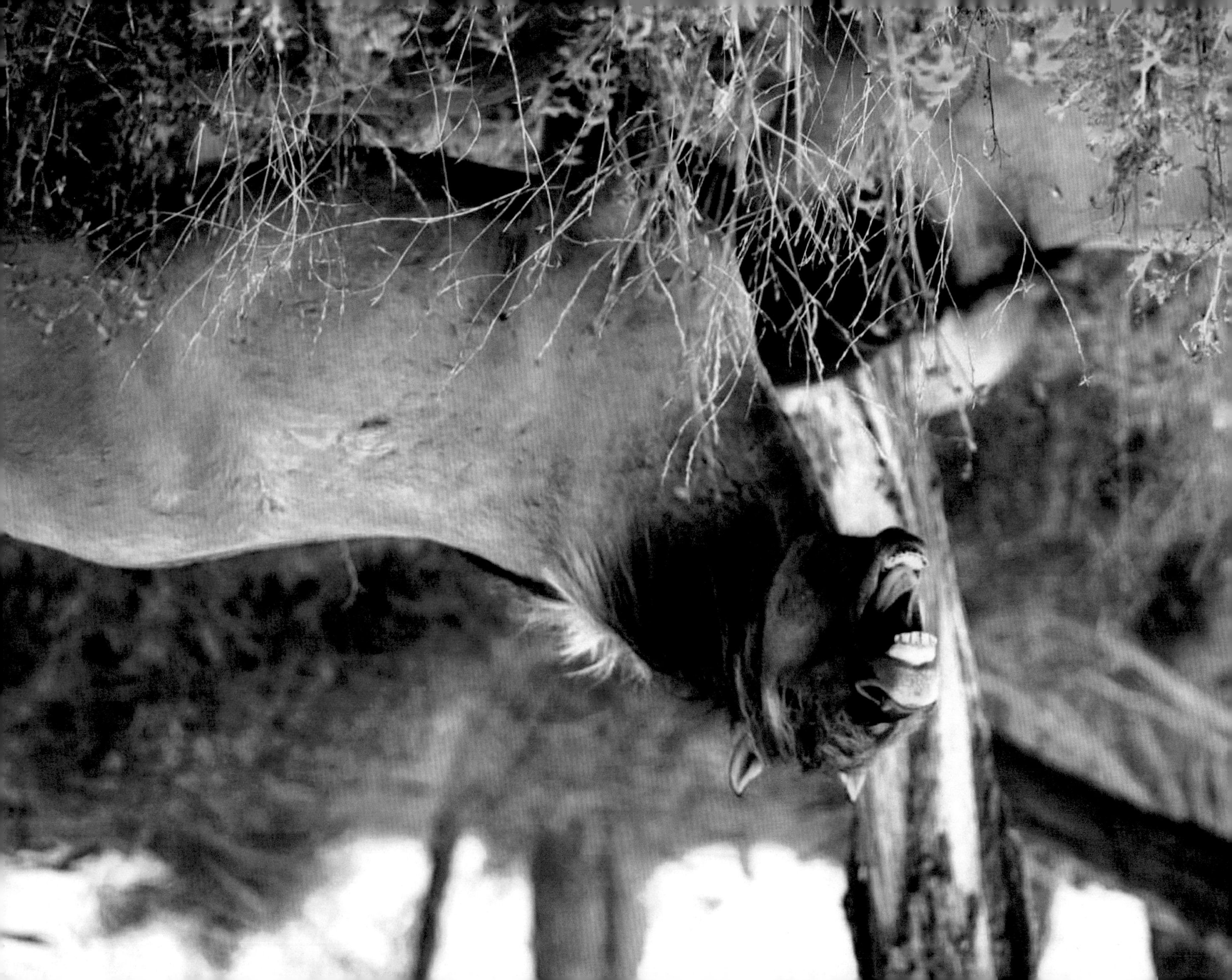

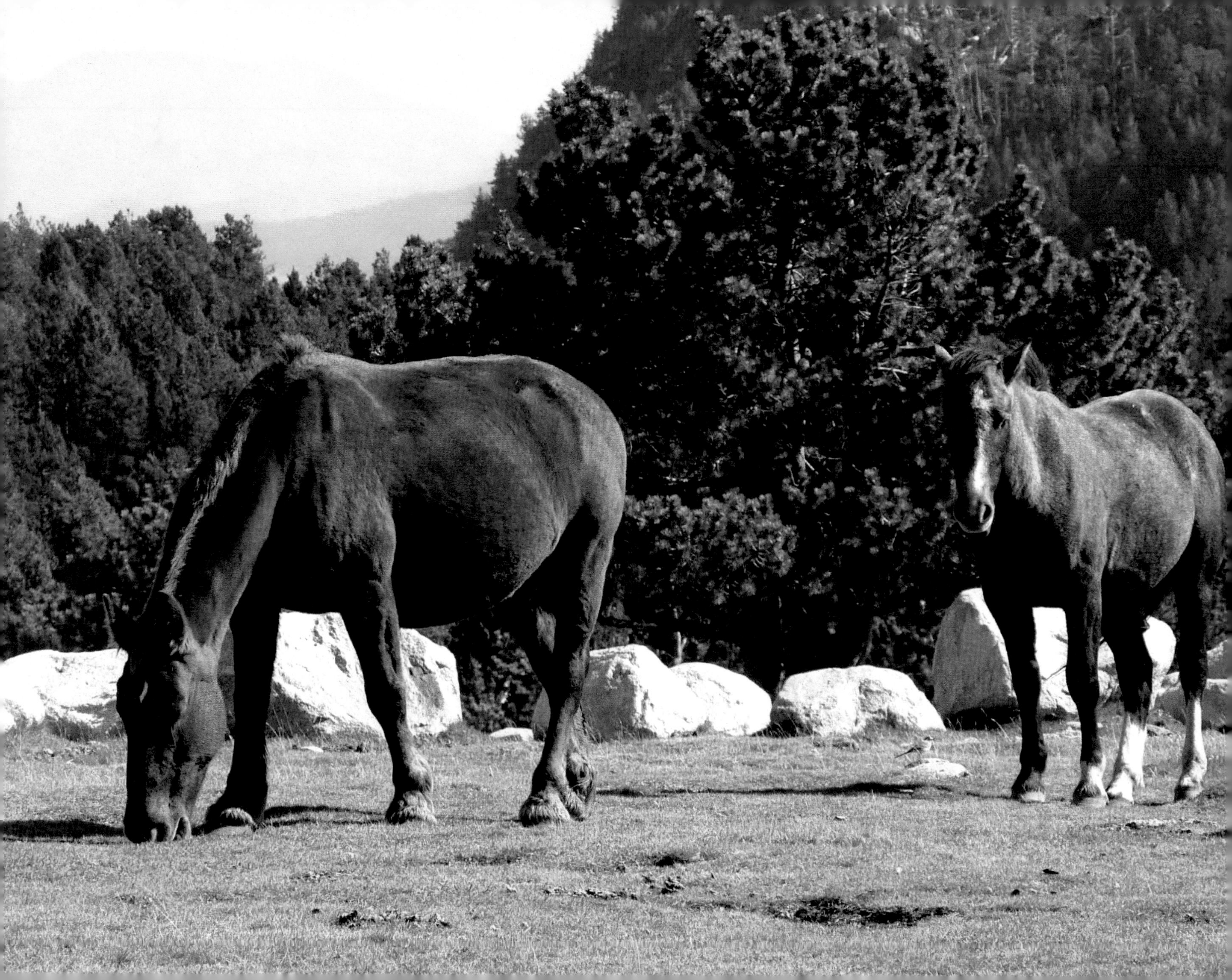

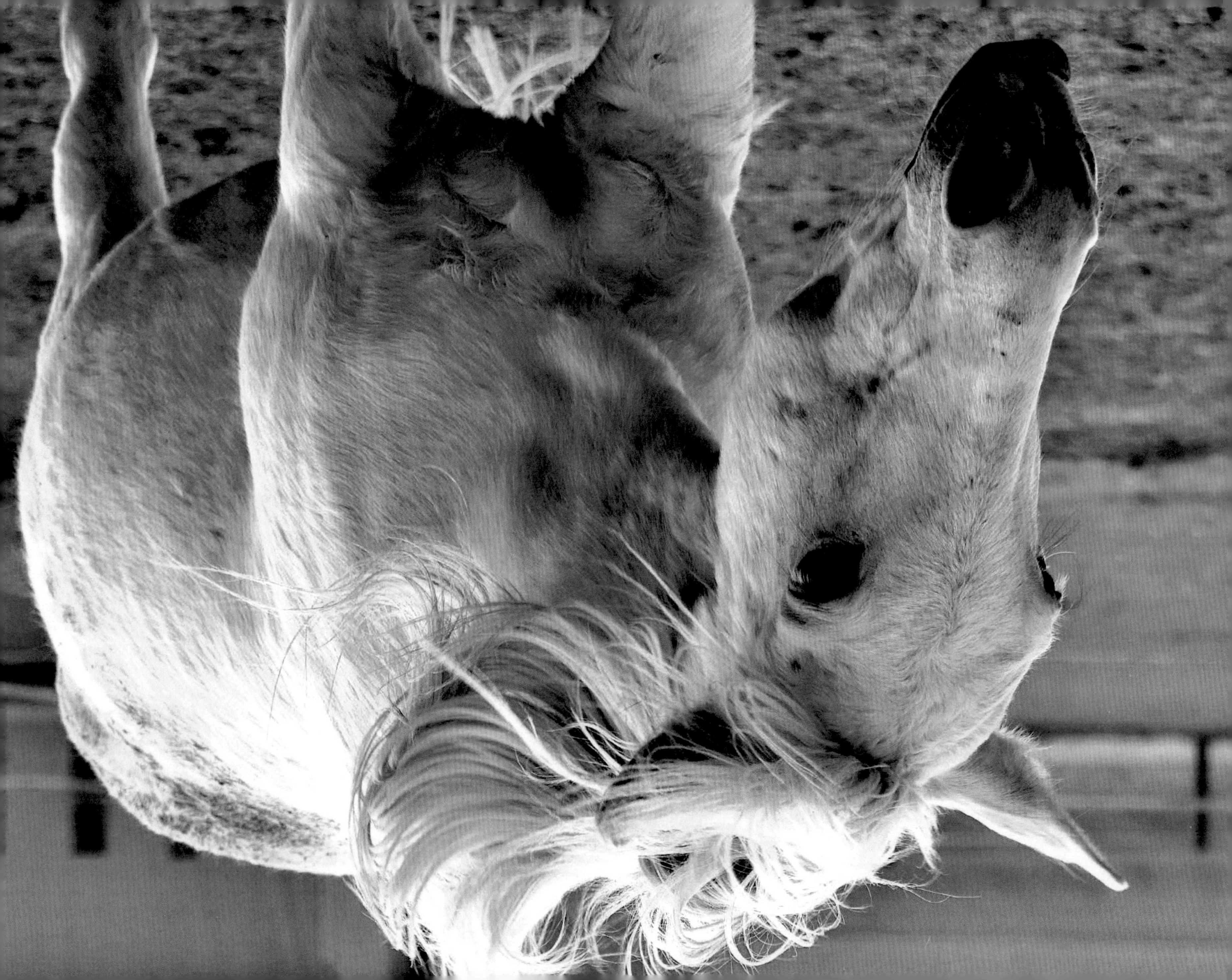

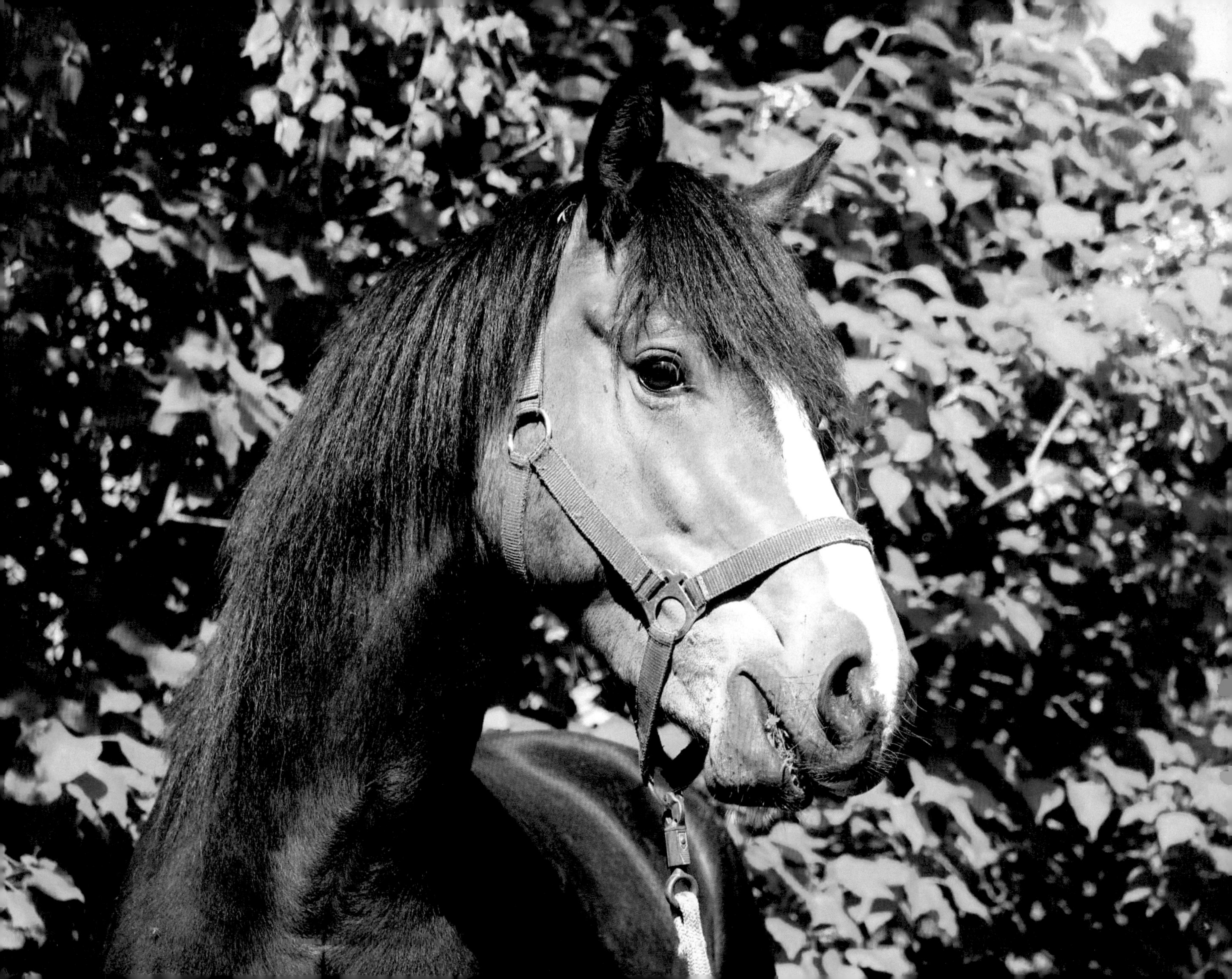

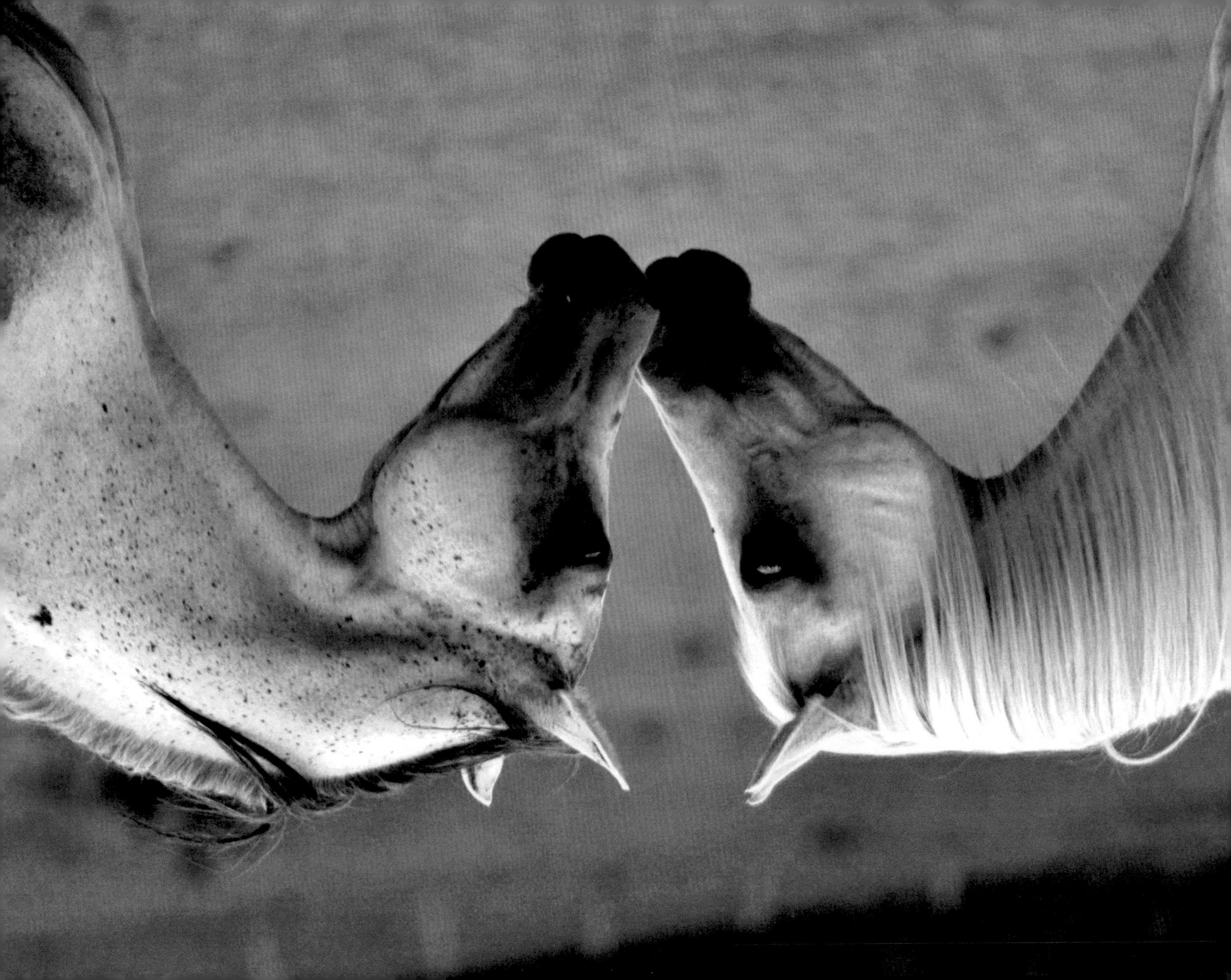